The Authentic Life

Also by Ezra Bayda

At Home in the Muddy Water: A Guide to Finding Peace within Everyday Chaos

Being Zen: Bringing Meditation to Life

Beyond Happiness: The Zen Way to Happiness

Zen Heart: Simple Advice for Living with Mindfulness and Compassion

The

Authentic Life

Zen Wisdom for Living Free from Complacency and Fear

Ezra Bayda

Shambhala • *Boston & London* • 2014

Shambhala Publications, Inc.
Horticultural Hall
300 Massachusetts Avenue
Boston, Massachusetts 02115
www.shambhala.com

9 8 7 6 5 4 3 2 1

First Edition
Printed in the United States of America

⊗This edition is printed on acid-free paper that meets the
American National Standards Institute Z39.48 Standard.
♻This book is printed on 30% postconsumer recycled paper.
For more information please visit www.shambhala.com.

Distributed in the United States by Random House, Inc.,
and in Canada by Random House of Canada Ltd

Designed by James D. Skatges

Library of Congress Cataloging-in-Publication Data

Bayda, Ezra.
The authentic life: Zen wisdom for living free from complacency
and fear/Ezra Bayda.—First Edition.
pages cm
ISBN 978-1-61180-092-0 (pbk.: alk. paper)
1. Spiritual life—Zen Buddhism. I. Title.
BQ9288.B393 2014
294.3'444—dc23
2013028425

This book is dedicated to Elizabeth Hamilton, my wife, fellow teacher and closest friend. Through our over twenty-one years together, and in spite of my blind spots and human frailties, she has been a constant source of support and encouragement. Particularly in this last and most difficult year, more than anything, it has been her love that has sustained me. It has also allowed me to see her and appreciate her in a new and more profound way.

Contents

PART ONE

The Territory and the Map

1. Skeletons at the Feast   3
2. The Rocky Road   10
3. The Eternal Recurrence   18
4. Doorways into Reality   26
5. Transforming Energy   38

PART TWO

Awakening the Mind

6. What about Happiness?   51
7. No One Special to Be   61
8. Who's Who in the Zoo?   71
9. The Misguided Quest   79
10. Shades of Gray   89

PART THREE

Emotional Awakening

11. The Dilemma of Anger   99
12. Saying Yes to Fear   112
13. The Great Teaching   123

Contents

14. What We Really Want   136
15. Sound Bites That Matter   145

PART FOUR

Awakening the Heart

16. The Bigger Picture   157
17. The Song of Meditation   166
18. The Most Important Thing   174
19. Enjoy the Ride   185

PART ONE

The Territory and the Map

I

Skeletons at the Feast

One of my first and abiding memories of of being woken up to the precariousness of life occurred when I was living in New York City in my early twenties: I read a newspaper story about a man shooting people on the street below from the roof of a high-rise. What affected me the most was the arbitrary nature of the deaths—you could be walking along and, without warning, be shot and killed, for no apparent reason. Over the years this sad theme has played out again and again—stories of individuals with guns going on a rampage at schools and workplaces, and even at movie theaters, killing people they don't even know.

Many of the books I've been reading recently have centered around events in Europe during World War II, again involving the theme of arbitrary death. There are numerous examples of the Gestapo shooting people almost on a whim, or breaking into a house in the middle of a holiday supper and five minutes later everyone in the entire family would be dead. In just a moment everything changes.

Or, a version closer to home, how we're all just one doctor's visit away from hearing that we, or someone close to us, has some life-altering condition. In Buddhism this theme is commonly described as the philosophy of impermanence, the objective fact that over time everything changes. I think of it more in terms of skating on thin ice, where we glide along on autopilot, going from one thing to another, pretending we have endless time. We're usually ignoring how thin beneath us the ice actually is; even though we know intellectually that we don't have endless time, we don't really believe it. We tend to ignore the fact that sooner or later there are things we'll all have to deal with—the inevitable shifts in our life circumstances that will trigger anxiety and uncertainty, such as our own declining health, or unexpected and unwanted changes in our finances or our relationships.

In other words, spiritual practice, in large part, involves learning how to respond to life's blows, including our own physical and emotional difficulties. A crucial step is to learn to see our difficulties as our path, as our opportunity. A simple truth that we can all experience for ourselves is that it is often our most painful experiences that lead us to deepened self-discovery, to growth, and even at times to freedom. The more we accept this truth, the more we can view our difficult situations as an opportunity—the opportunity to move out of our protected cocoon world, the opportunity to live in a more genuine way, the opportunity to truly appreciate this life. It's also good to be able to distinguish between difficulties that are real and those that are just creations of our own drama. A Holocaust survivor once said, "There's a big difference between a lump in our oatmeal and a lump in our breast." All too often we confuse the two. But when the lump in the breast arises, we need to know what to do.

Please be clear that this isn't about worrying about or expecting bad things to happen. That would be simply indulging in negative imaginings, which is the opposite of spiritual practice. This is about honestly acknowledging the things we don't want to look at—opening to the fears that none of us want to face. Yet, paradoxically, facing these fears allows us to come closer to truly appreciating the life that we have, just as it is.

One of the World War II books I recently read was a novel called *Skeletons at the Feast*. The title caught me immediately, although I honestly didn't know what it meant. One interpretation of the phrase "skeletons at the feast" refers to the ancient Roman practice of bringing an actual skeleton to the big feasts, to remind people to seize the day, or, as the phrase goes, "Eat, drink, and be merry, for tomorrow you may die." This sentiment may have some merit, but mostly, as you probably have experienced for yourself, it can easily lead to a life of desire, grasping, and ultimately dissatisfaction.

Another interpretation of the phrase "skeletons at the feast" is that it describes a life of waking sleep. We sleepwalk through life as skeletons—anxious, confused, and unhappy, even though we're in the midst of the feast of life, the life of wonder and genuine appreciation. A quote from the Bible sheds some light on this: "It is harder for a rich man to pass into the kingdom of heaven than it is for a camel to pass through the eye of a needle." In other words, when we live the complacent life of sleep, going from one thing to another as if we have endless time, we have little chance of enjoying the feast of living a genuine life of awareness—the life we're in the midst of right now.

Dostoyevsky once said, "Suffering is the sole origin of consciousness." Many believe this—that unless we're hurting, we'll never make the efforts that are required in order to wake up from the life of waking sleep. Does this mean we have to lead a life of suffering in order to enter the kingdom? Is it necessary to fall through the cracks in the thin ice? It's certainly true that many of us enter the spiritual path because we are suffering. When we feel the thin ice beneath us—the anxious quiver, the loneliness, the alienation—we naturally want relief. For me, in my early twenties, it was the constant state of anxiety and fear that drove me to spiritual practice, and my main motivation was wanting to be free from the unending discomfort. It's worthwhile for each of us to reflect on our own situation and on what brought us to spiritual practice, and specifically what we were trying to get away from—where we felt bad and wanted relief.

In a way, don't we assume we have to suffer? It's a basic tenet of both Christianity and Judaism, so it's very much embedded in our cultural way of seeing the world. It's also the First Noble Truth in Buddhist teaching—that life is suffering. Perhaps this is true, that the shocks of life, and our difficulties in the areas of our health, our financial security, or our relationships are what drive us to spiritual practice. But perhaps it is not always true, or at least it is not the whole truth. For example, we can be quite happy in conventional terms—having good health, a good job and relationship—and still feel that something is not quite right. It's not that we're suffering in the usual sense, or trying to get relief from our life, but there's still a feeling that something is missing. In other words, there is a basic unsatisfactoriness that pervades throughout. This is the experience of feeling disconnected from ourselves, disconnected from the heart. So even when a person is not suffering in the normal sense, this sense of existential disconnectedness will often lead one in the direction of spiritual practice. This is the quality that's called aspiration— our genuine desire to connect, or you could say to find God, or to find our authentic way.

The problem is it's very easy to get caught in a myopic, or

Me-centered, view of spiritual practice, and lose sight of our authentic way. A major part of the problem is that we identify with such a narrow part of who we are—that is, our small self, where we identify with our thoughts, our stories, our dramas, our bodies. We live out of the deep-seated illusion that we need to *be* a particular way and, even more so, that we need to *feel* a particular way, such as peaceful or comfortable or in control. As a result, we miss out on the freedom of connecting with a bigger sense of Self—of who we most truly are. In fact, the fundamental problem that prevents us from living authentically is that we're disconnected from our true self.

Finding our authentic way doesn't mean we have to have a deep realization of the connectedness of all and everything. We can find it in increments, starting with the understanding that every event in our life can be seen as part of the path to awakening. When spiritual practice begins to become the central orientation of our life, when we increasingly remember to ask ourselves, "Can I see this situation as my path?"—then we are in the process of living most authentically.

The point is that it's sometimes good to look at what drives our practice, to see where we're motivated primarily by wanting to alleviate our distress, to make our life more comfortable and safe; and conversely, where we're driven by our aspiration to live genuinely, to reconnect with our most authentic self. A good question to occasionally ask ourselves is, "How can I feed my aspiration without turning it into just one more form of grasping?"

For example, we can read books that feed the part of us that wants to live more genuinely. I mentioned that I've been reading a number of very moving novels—accounts of people's struggles during the time of World War II. And interestingly, although there was no mention of spiritual practice as I would normally understand it, the books nonetheless touched me in a way that feeds the desire to awaken. More specifically, because the events are so evocatively described, one feels as if one is actually living and suffering through them. As a consequence, they've deepened my compassion for the very real suffering that so many people have gone through.

Each of our experiences is like "food" for our spiritual growth. Just as the food we eat can either nourish or deplete the physical body, so can our everyday experiences nourish or deplete our spiritual growth. Do we want to feed the small mind and continue living like a skeleton at the feast, or do we want to feed our aspiration, our Big Self? I believe the kind of food we get from reading certain books and perhaps seeing certain films, although certainly not enough by itself, is nonetheless invaluable on our path. It can remind us and deepen our aspiration to awaken.

We have to continually reflect on what we're doing, to recall what we truly aspire to. At bottom, the heart that seeks to awaken, to live genuinely, is more real than anything. It is the nameless drive that calls us to be who we most truly are. When we are not in touch with this, we feel the existential anxiety of disconnection. In order to reconnect, perhaps more than anything we must cultivate honesty in seeing how we skate on the thin ice of life, ignoring the fears we don't want to deal with while pretending that we have endless time.

As we feed and cultivate our aspiration, we gradually develop a sense of purpose—that is, a bigger view of what our life is about. Without this sense of purpose it's very difficult to actually commit to truly living genuinely rather than just gliding along on autopilot from one thing to another, driven primarily by the desires for comfort, security, control, and approval. One way to help develop a sense of purpose is to reflect on who we most admire and ask ourselves what qualities we see in them that are most inspiring to us. These are the very qualities within us that are calling out to reach fruition. These are the qualities that inspire us to become who we most truly are. We may be moved by another's kindness, or their ability to be appreciative, or by their seriousness of purpose, or sense of presence and inner quiet. As we reflect on these qualities, they feed our aspiration. Just as our difficulties can push us in our spiritual quest, our aspiration can elevate us and pull us. This dual motivation is what is required to help us find our authentic way.

It may also be helpful to experience what author and long-time spiritual practitioner Lewis Richmond calls "Lightning Strikes." This is the moment when we realize deeply that we won't be here forever. Of course, when experiencing a moment like this we can easily sink into despair and regret. But it's also possible to use these moments as a wake-up and to see them as a doorway into living in a more open and genuine way. We don't have to continue living like skeletons at the feast. When we find our own way, we can understand Wu-men's famous line: "When the mind isn't clouded by unnecessary things, this is the best moment of your life."

2

The Rocky Road

Following the path of spiritual practice is bound at times to be a rocky road, filled with obstacles and detours. Some are of our own making, based in our individual psychology and conditioning. For example, if we're prone to procrastination or to seeking diversions, this will surely impact our practice. So will the tendency to be a perfectionist. However, there are other obstacles that seem to be universal, and it is almost inevitable that these will be encountered along the practice path. Interestingly, if we don't recognize how these obstacles and detours manifest in our lives, the practice path becomes much rockier and more difficult to traverse. There are three obstacles in particular that we need to address.

1. Not Understanding the Power of Waking Sleep

The first obstacle on the practice path is misunderstanding the magnitude of what is called "waking sleep," and not recognizing the power of its impact on practice. The term "waking sleep" describes the state in which we spend most of our waking hours—where we are identified, or lost in, whatever is happening. For example, we may be so identified with our thoughts that we rarely question whether they are true. In fact, quite often we're not even aware that we're thinking; yet our thoughts are the veil though which we perceive reality, and they certainly dictate how we feel and act. Our thoughts are not the only integral part of waking sleep—we seem to be equally addicted to our emotions. Even when our emotions are unpleasant, as when we're irritated, we nonetheless often prefer to indulge them.

Waking sleep is also characterized by being completely identified with our activities. We can be so lost in what we're doing that hours can go by without much actual awareness. In fact, it is this lack of awareness that is the most significant aspect of waking sleep. We're rarely present for more than a few moments at a time—most of our waking moments are spent lost in or identified with our thoughts, emotions, and behaviors. In a way we exist primarily as sleepwalkers, rarely having the sustained state of presence that is part of being more awake.

This description may sound quite pessimistic, and at odds with how some traditions emphasize our basic goodness. Buddhism, for example, teaches that we're born with our true nature fully intact and that our spiritual aspiration is to allow our true nature to reveal itself, just as an acorn aspires to become an oak tree. Yet emphasizing our basic goodness, as important as it is, is only part of the picture. No matter how strong our aspiration may be, if we don't develop deep insight into the power and magnitude of waking sleep, we will be blindsided by it again and again.

It's imperative for us to understand that spiritual practice is not just something we do when we're sitting in meditation or when we're attending a spiritual retreat. Because of the pervasive and unrelenting nature of waking sleep, living a life of spiritual practice means practicing with *everything* we encounter, not just with meditation techniques or when something upsets us. The more we include in our practice life, the more satisfying our life can be; if we neglect seeing *whatever arises* as an opportunity for practice, it greatly limits our possibilities for inner growth. Whatever we exclude from practice guarantees that we'll stay stuck where we are, which eventually leads to frustration and disappointment—perhaps even to giving up on practice, or on ourselves.

2. UNDERESTIMATING RESISTANCE

The second obstacle we encounter in practice, closely related to the first, is underestimating the degree to which resistance is a predictable and inevitable part of a practice life. Resistance is not the same thing as being passive or lazy. We can be busy and productive and still be quite resistant—resistant in the sense that we don't want to honestly look at ourselves and what we're doing. Resistance comes in many forms: not wanting to sit in meditation, choosing to spin off into our mental world, suppressing or avoiding emotional pain, finding fault with ourselves, finding fault with others. Another, more subtle form of resistance is thinking and talking about practice rather than actually experiencing our life. Thinking and talking about practice is an easy substitute for the real efforts that a practice life requires. They allow us to avoid the anxious quiver inside.

Wanting life to be other than it is seems to be the most basic form of resistance. We don't like the fact that life is not subject to our control and that it is always changing. We resist facing our life as it is because that would mean abandoning our sense of entitlement to safety, control, and comfort. This is not a small thing. As we observe ourselves, we'll see that there's a big part of us that really doesn't want to wake up to life as it is. We have to be honest about this. We want to hold on to our beliefs and, in a way, even to our suffering. It's a sad fact that we don't want to give up our habits and illusions even when they make us miserable, in part because we cling to the familiar. We spend much of our lives trying to just get along, hoping for our little share of happiness. Unfortunately, this guarantees that we'll end up living primarily from the smallness of our attachments and from the slavery to our fears.

Resistance can be seen as the ego's effort to maintain control. We can see our resistance in virtually everything we do: in resisting effort and change, in not wanting to stay with our experience for more than a few seconds, in spinning off into thinking about the past or the future. We can see this resistance in our commitment to believing such thoughts as "This is too hard," "I can't do it," "I'm unworthy." Yet no matter what form it takes, resistance brings us no peace.

We will particularly resist certain feelings and experiences— the ones that make us feel the most uncomfortable. This is our "edge," the place beyond which we're presently unwilling to go. The point is that it is in turning away from our own edge that we make it seem so solid. Whatever we resist will continue to exert a strong hold on us. But when we cultivate the willingness to be with life just as it is, our relationship to what we've avoided starts to change. As we begin to see through the solidity of our resistance, our lives become more fluid and workable, enabling us to move beyond where we were once stuck. Even if we don't like our life as it is, we don't have to wage war against it. We can start meeting our resistance squarely by first noticing all of the ways that we avoid the present moment, all of the ways we avoid practice, all of the ways we resist life as it is. And then, to practice with resistance, we need to simply *feel what it is*. If resistance is our experience in the present moment, we can explore it with the mind of curiosity. What does it actually feel like to resist? What is the actual physical experience in the body? The practice is to feel it—feel it fully. Clearly, understanding the depth of our resistance is of major importance in practice.

Another important aspect of resistance shows up when we hit "the dry spot," the place where we lose our connection with the aspiration that originally brought us to practice. Often we hit the dry spot when our expectations of practice are unfulfilled—when practice isn't bringing us the immediate peace, calm, or freedom from fear that we had hoped for. Disappointment can lead to anger, and anger to resistance.

The dry spot can come in different ways. For some it comes early on, as when students aren't motivated to set up a regular meditation routine. Others may suddenly hit a very solid wall, even though they've been meditating daily for many months or years. It's important to understand that vacillating between aspiration and resistance is the natural rhythm of practice, and the dry spot is a predictable manifestation of this natural cycle. But the first few times we hit it, the dry spot doesn't seem natural at all. In fact, we may believe that we're failing at practice, since the thoughts that arise in these moments seem like fixed truths: "I'm just wasting my time," "We're all just fooling ourselves," "I'll never be good at this." It's hard to see these thoughts for what they are: automatic reactions based on the natural ups and downs of the practice life.

Often when students hit a dry spot, they even leave practice. But if we can wait it out, we begin to understand these natural cycles of resistance. We even come to *expect* that the doubting mind will arise. We can learn that doubt in itself is not the problem; the problem comes from identifying with this small doubting self as who we really are. Doubt can even lead to a deepening of our quest—as long as we don't get lost in the negative beliefs that fuel it. For example, we can learn to use doubt as an opportunity to experience the grief of our unfulfilled dreams. We can learn to surrender to, and reside in, the physical experience of what doubt feels like in the body, instead of following the story line of negative thoughts. Not following the story line can be difficult, because the thoughts seem so real, so solid, so compelling. But as we stay with the visceral experience of doubt itself, even as the confusion of not knowing remains, the dryness is transfused with a deeper sense of aspiration. Thomas Merton expressed this clearly: "True love and prayer are learned in the moment when prayer has become impossible and the heart has turned to stone." When we understand the cycles of resistance, and when we can wait out a dry period by resting in the direct physical experience of doubt, we will gradually come to feel a sense of renewed direction.

3. WANTING TO FEEL A PARTICULAR WAY

The third major obstacle we encounter on the spiritual path is our deep-seated desire to feel a particular way, whether it's calm or clear or spacious or simply free of anxiety. This obstacle is so universal and so deeply entrenched that we are guaranteed to get stuck in it again and again. In fact, whenever we feel frustrated in any way, if we simply ask, "How is it supposed to be?"—we'll see that our discomfort is based, at least in part, on the entitled belief that we *should* feel different, namely better. Probably all of us share the illusion that if we practice long enough and hard enough, we'll get what we want—enlightenment, good health, a satisfying relationship, or whatever else we're seeking. The hope is that in getting the reward, we will then feel the way we want to feel, and be happy.

We can tell that we're still harboring this illusion if we believe that not feeling good or experiencing distress means that something is wrong—or even that something is wrong with *us*. This persistent belief drives us to do whatever we can to alleviate our discomfort. We think if we just practice harder, we're sure to feel better. We should never underestimate the extent to which we equate feeling better with being awake. But a key point about spiritual practice is that we don't have to feel *any* particular way.

The only way we can learn this essential point is from our own life experience. It took me months of struggling with an intense immune system illness to learn that it was possible to experience genuine equanimity even in the midst of persistent bodily discomfort, including unrelenting bouts of nausea. The equanimity came, in part, from seeing through the sense of entitlement, starting with the belief that we need to feel good in order to be happy. The lie that this entitlement tells us is that we can't be happy if we're in discomfort. But giving up this entitlement, what remains? The simple answer: life-as-it-is. This leads us to the basic conclusion that all we can do is experience, and work with, whatever is arising in our life right now. No matter what is going on or how we feel about it, the essence of spiritual practice is to honestly acknowledge what is happening in the moment and stay present with our experience of it. In this way we can come to feel a true appreciation for life just as it is, because we're no longer caught in our judgments or demands that life be different.

There's a famous Buddhist story about a man who was shot in the chest with an arrow. The pain was great, but the Buddha pointed out how much greater the man's pain would be if he had been shot with a second arrow in exactly the same spot. What this teaching suggests is that however painful or disappointing our experience may be, when we add the second arrow of our judgmental thoughts about it, we only deepen the pain, leading to greater suffering.

For example, if I wake up not feeling well and then add the judgment "This shouldn't be happening to me" on top of that, it will make me feel even worse. The countermeasure to our judgments is to move out of the mental world, based in our thoughts about what's happening, into what we're actually physically feeling in the present moment. Judgments are based in ideals or expectations, and these thought-based pictures are at least one step removed from what is real. Coming back to what is, minus our thought-based pictures, is a step toward freedom.

This obstacle—the deeply seated desire to feel a particular way—first has to be seen through. And then, as we realize that we don't have to feel a particular way in order to be free, we can experience the equanimity that comes with staying truly present with what is.

These three obstacles—misunderstanding the depth of waking sleep, underestimating resistance, and wanting to feel a particular way—are guaranteed to be encountered along the spiritual path. They are also sure to make the path of awakening a rocky one, at least for a time. However, knowing about them is the first step toward learning how to effectively work with them. And working with them, in turn, is a major step toward discovering what it means to live authentically.

3

The Eternal Recurrence

There's an old Zen saying: "Realizing the Way is hard. Once you have realized it, preserving it is hard. When you can preserve it, putting it into practice is hard."

When we realize how hard spiritual practice is, the initial honeymoon phase usually ends, especially if we believed that practice was going to save us from ourselves—from our fears and our distress. When we realize that our practice is not, in fact, going to ensure that we'll permanently feel a particular way— such as calm or clear or compassionate—it is very easy to get discouraged. Some students leave practice at this point. But for those who stick it out in spite of the discouragement, there can gradually come a dawning realization. Simone Weil put it very well, writing, "Even if our efforts of attention seem for years to be producing no result, one day a light that is in exact proportion to them will flood the soul."

We may not necessarily feel like a light is flooding our soul, but we nonetheless come to the undeniable realization that something is shifting. We begin to realize that every event in our life is an opportunity to practice—that every experience can be food for our being. With this understanding our sense of presence deepens and becomes a more natural part of our everyday reality. We also begin to observe that we don't react so quickly, and that when we do react, the reactions are not nearly as intense as they once were, nor do they last as long. And further, we come to realize that our thoughts are *just* thoughts, and that we don't have to believe them or act on them.

This is the process of gradual awakening, yet this isn't something that comes quickly or easily. There's a price to be paid for it—starting with daily efforts to be present, and continuing with a willingness to work with our everyday difficulties. We also see the need to commit to periodically attending retreats, in order to provide an opportunity to go deeper; and to learning the true meaning of perseverance, which involves continuing to make efforts regardless of the outcome, regardless of how we feel in the moment.

Sometimes we might wonder, "How does this process of gradual awakening actually work?" The short answer is: *awareness heals*. What this actually means is very difficult to describe, but there's a scientific phenomenon called "the observer effect" that can help explain the process. The observer effect is sometimes equated with a discovery of the famous physicist Werner Heisenberg, who said, "The very act of observing disturbs the system." He was describing how the light from a high-powered microscope actually alters that which is being observed. Likewise, the light of awareness alters and transforms our experience, including our experience of ourselves—the many "Me's" of our small self. The more we are aware of these small selves, the more our attachment to their opinions, entitlements, and fears begins to diminish. This is why knowing ourselves, with precision and honesty, is a time-honored path to becoming free of our conditioned patterns. While what *actually* happens during this process may still be a mystery, we can nonetheless discover for ourselves, from our own experience, that over time, awareness heals.

In the meantime, practice can seem very hard; and it's inevitable and predictable that we'll have periods of discouragement. Yet, even though we may, at times, get discouraged or confused, the real question is, what then? We can either succumb to the discouragement and confusion or we can ask ourselves, "How do I choose to live?" Occasionally we might think that the path of spiritual practice is too hard and want to give up. We may also reach a point in practice where we get stuck in a rut, to a large extent just going through the motions. At this point, we may fall into the assumption that practice is just about technique—such as proper posture and feeling the breath—and forget the *point* of spiritual practice, which includes learning to live as genuinely as possible.

It's very easy to forget the point of whatever we've been trying to do, where we lose contact with any bigger sense of meaning. This can be very perplexing, and we may find that we simply refuse to do what we know is best for us. The choice of ignoring what's best for us is certainly not logical. But if we look at our own life, perhaps we can understand it better. When we get discouraged or stuck in some way, how often have we been paralyzed with inertia and fear of making a choice? Perhaps we question whether to stay in a relationship or a job. Or we may feel stuck in our practice, unwilling or unable to commit to meditating every day, or not remembering the need to work with what's right in front of us that's calling for attention.

We don't do what we know will help us live more genuinely, in part because of habit—the inertia of continuing to do the same things almost mechanically. We can add to that the fact that we are often just too lazy to exert a particular type of effort. We prefer the false comfort of our busyness and diversions, the false comfort of our planning and fantasizing, even the false comfort of our emotions. With anger, for example, we prefer the false comfort of being right—the juiciness and power of it. Or in the case of our fears—as much as we dislike them, we still prefer the false comfort of the familiar. We stay trapped in our fear-based cocoon world rather than entering into the potentially healing, unknown territory of actually being present with our fears. The same is true of depression: we prefer the numbness of the depression to actually feeling the feelings that our depression is helping us avoid.

Does this make sense? On one level it doesn't, in that we're choosing to hold on to a very small life—a life of complacency, rather than living more genuinely. This is primarily because we're so identified with our small self—that is, with our deeply held beliefs and our little dramas. We've forgotten the bigger point of what we're doing. We should never underestimate the forces of resistance and inertia—of being stuck in habits and entitlements, such as the belief that life should be free from discomfort. We may also become stuck in deeply rooted thoughts, such as "This is too hard—I can't do it." When we get caught in the small mind, where we're forgetting the point, or particularly where we're doubting ourselves and questioning what we should do, there's an excellent practice question we can ask ourselves. I learned this from the nineteenth-century existential philosopher Friedrich Nietzsche, whom, in a way, I consider my first teacher. He posed the doctrine of the eternal recurrence, where *we hypothesize a reality in which everything in our life recurs again and again and again, in exactly the way we are living it now, throughout eternity.*

Please note: this is a hypothetical position—we don't need to consider it as a true statement about reality. The point is, when faced with a decision about how to live our life, can we make use of this doctrine by simply raising the question, "What would I do in this situation if I had to live my life in the exact same way, over and over and over again, throughout eternity?" This question can be disconcerting, because it will no doubt bring up many of our fears—such as our fear of failure, or our fear of the unfamiliar. It can also bring up our fear of living dishonestly, disconnected from our true self.

This question may sound similar to asking, "What would I do if I had one year, or one week, or one day, to live?" Actually, the two questions are quite different. If we thought we had a very short time to live, there would be fewer consequences to what we decided to do—we could quit our job, run off to Paris or Tahiti, spend all of our money, and so on. But with the question of eternal recurrence, the decision about what to do is all about recurring consequences—of repeating our exact behaviors and attitudes for eternity.

Answering this question is not just about making changes in our behavior. It's more about becoming who we truly are. When we take this question seriously, we are forced to look at ourselves with a penetrating honesty. We may also be forced to face the fears that hold us back from living from our true heart, because reflecting on the question of eternal recurrence will include actions *not* taken, the choices we avoid. When we ask the question, the remorse of an *unlived* life will gnaw at us. Through the struggle between the yes and the no—the yes ("I wish to live more honestly and awake") and the no ("I want to resist")—we're making the conscious effort to go against our fears and our deeply conditioned patterns. It is through this conscious effort that something transforms in our being.

In challenging our small mind—the mind based in complacency, entitlements, and fear—we are making a commitment to living in the most authentic way. We are also opening the doorway to reality, where our true self is no longer just a vague concept. For example, when I started to think about writing this book, which is my sixth, many doubts and questions began to arise. Does the world really need another book? Do I really have something worthwhile to say? Will it be well received? The small mind had a field day feeding the voices of self-doubt. These were familiar voices, and I didn't really believe them, but they nonetheless had a toehold and caused me to hesitate. Asking the question of the eternal recurrence—"If I had to live my life over again an eternal number of times in the exact same way, would I write this book?"—allowed me to bypass the little mind of self-judgment. It reminded me that the point of writing wasn't to try to sound good or to receive praise, but instead to simply focus on the fact that there were things that I truly wanted to say, things that have been essential in my own practice. I also realized that I don't write just to articulate what I already know; I write to help uncover my genuine life. The question of the eternal recurrence reminded me to not play it safe or be defended but instead to try to live as authentically as possible.

For the question of the eternal recurrence to become real, and to help you to truly commit to your life, you have to actually raise the question, preferably in a specific situation. Think of a current area where you're trying to decide what to do, where you feel stuck or at your edge, and want to know how to move forward in your life. Now ask, "Would I want to deal with this, in this way, innumerable times more?" This is often not an easy question to answer. Moreover, you may not like the answer, because it may mean that you have to face something you don't want to face. For example, if your primary reason for staying in a relationship is because you fear being alone, once you ask whether you would truly want to live this life repeatedly in the exact same way, the obvious answer of "No!" might be very frightening. But remember, to leave a situation like this would not just be about changing your behavior—it would push you to summon the courage to do the *exact* thing that you most needed to do to grow and to live most authentically, namely to face your loneliness. However, in some situations you may have to accept that in the moment, you just don't care whether or not you stay stuck. But ultimately, if you want to pursue practice honestly, that is, if you want to live your life most genuinely, this can be a very useful guideline.

Keep in mind that it's a given that practice is hard and that efforts are required for a long time. But if you're sincere and persevere, you'll gradually experience your life in a new way— with more presence, more openness, less reactivity. This will no doubt entail working with periods of confusion and discouragement, and occasionally being confronted with making a choice of how you want to live your life. Then you can ask the question of the eternal recurrence, which is another way of asking, "Do I want to stay stuck in complacency and fear, or do I want to follow the path of living from a more open heart?"

Remember, we get stuck because we've lost touch with a bigger sense of things. We forget that our stuck place is not an obstacle but rather our exact path to freedom. Yet this is only true if we're willing to bring awareness to it. We also need to remember that awareness heals. This, however, requires that we make the choice, the effort, to actually be aware. We may know this intellectually, but when the small mind takes over, we can quickly forget.

When we ask the question of the eternal recurrence, and can listen to the Big Mind as it guides us past our small-minded patterns and fears, it allows us to say yes to our life—even our difficulties and pain—because we understand that the joy would not have been possible without the pain. All of the pains, as well as our mistakes, our weaknesses, our attachments, are a necessary part of our development. All of those things we have so disliked have nonetheless pushed us in our growth, and are a necessary part of the whole interweaving tapestry of where we stand in the present moment. In answering the call of the eternal recurrence we are, in effect, saying yes to all of it, willingly affirming our commitment and direction. This is the direct path to becoming who we truly are. As the artist Odilon Redon said, "With my eyes more widely opened upon things, I learned that the life that we have can also reveal joy."

4

Doorways into Reality

As we glide along on the thin ice of life, just going from one thing to another, pretending that we have endless time, sooner or later we are bound to fall through one of the cracks in the thin ice. When we do, we usually quickly scramble to find some strategy to help regain the illusion of control. Here's an example: On a recent trip to the former prison on Alcatraz Island I had the fascinating experience of walking through its halls, standing in the cells, and imagining what it would have been like to be confined there. Before Alcatraz was closed as a functioning prison, it was unique in that it kept all of its prisoners isolated in solitary cells. I heard the story of one prisoner who was put into a pitch-black solitary cell as punishment. He ripped a button off his shirt and threw it in the air, then got on his knees to look for it. Then he'd throw it again. Falling through the thin ice—in this case into the terror of a dark cell—he would throw the button again and again just to avoid going crazy in the dark.

This example may sound like it has nothing to do with us,

but the fact is we all have our own ways of avoiding the dark and our own strategies for throwing buttons. Ours may look more sane and more productive, but they're still attempts to avoid facing our own difficulties. Trying to avoid what's unpleasant seems to be deeply ingrained in the human psyche. After all, when life feels out of sync, we naturally seek comfort and relief. But the feeling that life is out of sync is hardly new; as Buddha pointed out more than 2,500 years ago, we'll always have to deal with the fact that life entails discomfort and disappointment. We will always have our many problems—concerns about financial security, relationship difficulties, fears about our health, anxious striving toward success and acceptance, and so on. Yet perhaps the most basic problem is that *we don't really want to have any problems*; perhaps that's a large part of what makes our current time seem so distressing to us.

Many people come to meditation-based practices with the expectation that these practices will calm them down and relieve the feelings of distress. Certainly meditation can do this to some extent; however, when we're knee-deep in emotional distress, it's not always likely that we'll remember to use these tools. Even if we could remember to meditate, simply sitting down to follow the breath without directly addressing our difficulties is unlikely to bring a deep or lasting peace to the mind. The difficulties remain.

Sometimes, when emotions are particularly intense and we feel the very uncomfortable feelings of groundlessness and helplessness, it is especially difficult to remember what we know. There's a good reason for this; when we're distressed, the "new," or conceptual, brain tends to stop working. This is called "cognitive shock," and it turns off the cognitive mind's basic ability to function. When the thinking brain is on sabbatical, we simply can't think clearly. During cognitive shock, the "old" brain, which is based on survival and defense, takes over. At this point we're likely to attack, withdraw, or go numb, none of which are conducive to awareness. To be honest, when caught in cognitive shock, we're fortunate if we can even remember that we want to be awake.

When clarity becomes obscured by the dark and swirling energy of emotional distress, it is sometimes necessary to do something as basic as taking several deep relaxing breaths, which help put us back in contact with the cognitive part of the brain. We do this by breathing in through the nose, then exhaling with long, slow breaths through the mouth. These relaxing breaths tend to subdue the old-brain response of panic and anxiety and allow us to reengage the mind of clarity. However, we may still be a little confused about what to do next, so it's very useful to have some concise reminders to bring us back to reality. The real question is, what helps us awaken? The answer to this overarching question can be broken down into five very straightforward and specific smaller questions, each of which is a doorway into reality.

1. "What Is Going On Right Now?"

This simply requires honestly acknowledging the objective situation. But to do this, we have to be able to see the difference between our reaction to what is happening and the actual facts of the situation. For instance, when we experience the panic of losing our job or seeing our investments disappear overnight, it is easy to get so caught up in our fears that we lose all sense of perspective. But what is actually happening in the present moment? Aren't we usually hijacked by the thoughts we've added, of the impending doom of homelessness or hunger, rather than actually experiencing homelessness or hunger? Clearly seeing our believed thoughts—which are often based in negative imaginings about the future—allows us to come back to the objective reality of what is happening.

Another example: When we're caught in the swirl of emotional distress, we almost always add the thought "Something is wrong"—either wrong in general or, more likely, wrong with another person or with ourselves. In addition, we will almost always think about how to escape from the distress—through trying to fix the situation or through blaming or analyzing. In short, working effectively with our emotional difficulties requires that we first see clearly not only what is actually happening but also what we're adding to the situation through our emotional reactions and escapes.

How much of our distress is rooted in the stories we weave around our experiences? Dropping our story line is critical to being aware of what is actually happening in the present moment. We need to see the story line for what it is and stop rehashing it over and over with our believed thoughts, since all they do is sustain and solidify our painful experiences. This is especially true when we are self-justifying and blaming. Asking the first practice question—"What is going on right now?"—can help us get out of the toxic loop of our stories.

2. "Can I See This as My Path?"

If we don't ask this crucial question, we're unlikely even to remember that this is our opportunity to awaken. Yet it is essential that we understand that our distressful situation is exactly what we need to work with in order to be free. For example, the person we find most irritating becomes a mirror, reflecting back to us exactly where we're stuck. After all, the irritation is what we add.

It is absolutely fundamental that we learn that when difficult situations and feelings arise, they are not obstacles to be avoided; instead these very difficulties are, in fact, the path itself. They're our opportunity to wake up out of our little protected world; they're our opportunity to awaken into a more authentic way of living. This point can't be overemphasized.

Of course, you may have heard this idea before—that our difficulties are our path. But it's a lot easier to understand this intellectually than it is to remember it when we're in the middle of the muddiness of life. Why? Because, again, we instinctively want a life that is problem-free. So we usually continue seeking comfort and safety until at some point, if we're fortunate, we get disappointed enough by life's blows to realize that our strategies—controlling, trying harder, withdrawing, blaming, whatever they are—will never give us the quality of life that all of us want. At that point—with life's disappointments as our teacher—we can start to use our difficulties as part of our path to awakening. Remembering the importance of this allows us to make the critical practice step of welcoming our distress, because we understand that as long as we continue resisting our experience, we will stay stuck.

3. "What Is My Most Believed Thought?"

Answering this is like taking a snapshot of the mind. It's tempting to skip over this question, especially since we often take our opinions as truth, even though our opinions in any given moment can be dependent on factors such as what we ate, what the weather is, or how we feel physically. This is what it means to live out of the subjective experience of "Me."

Even though observation of the mind allows us to see our superficial or surface thoughts with clarity, the deepest beliefs often stay below the surface, making it difficult to see what we're really believing. Thus, these deep-seated beliefs often dictate how we feel and act, and they continue to run almost unconsciously.

For example, deeply believed thoughts about our personal insecurity may not be evident on the surface in a given situation; truthfully, we're often unaware of their presence. But their toxic footprint often manifests itself in our anger, blame, depression, and shame. These deeply believed yet well-hidden thoughts of insecurity thus act like radar, and we often seek out experiences that confirm that our beliefs are true—the classic self-fulfilling prophecy. For example, if you believe that life is not safe, all you have to do is get a bill that's a little bit bigger than you expected, and your mind will start weaving scenarios of doom. Yet living with this radar constantly engaged means living in the past, not in the present.

We have to know where we get stuck in our particular radar-like beliefs. We also have to know how to work with them. The process begins with asking yourself, "What is my most believed thought?" However, if the answer doesn't come, you drop it and return to your physical experience rather than trying to figure it out with the mind. Then, a little while later, you ask the question again. Sooner or later, with perseverance, an answer will present itself, sometimes with an "aha!" quality.

For instance, your surface thought may be, "No one should have to put up with this." This thought expresses the protective voice of anger and frustration. But when we go deeper, we may discover a more strongly held thought, such as "I can't do this." It may even be revealed with the "aha!" of discovery. Then, as we get to know ourselves, we are no longer so surprised. Haven't we seen this belief many times before? It's at this point that our investment in our deeply seated negative beliefs about ourselves begins to diminish. But to get to this place, first we must inquire into what our most believed thoughts are.

4. "What Is This?"

This question, perhaps the most important one, can't be answered by the thinking mind. The actual answer comes from entering directly into the immediate, physical experience of the present moment. Right now, ask yourself, "What is this?" This question can apply to whatever the present moment holds, whether or not you feel any distress. Become aware of your physical posture. Feel the overall quality of the physical sensations in the body. Feel the tension in the face, chest, and stomach. Include awareness of the environment—the temperature, the quality of light, the surrounding sounds.

Ask the question again, "What is this?" Feel the body breathing in and out as you experience this felt sense of the moment. Beyond thoughts, what is it that experiences? Feel the energy in the body as you focus on the "whatness" (rather than the "whyness") of your experience. Only by doing this will you be able to answer the question, "What is this?"

Admittedly, it is difficult to maintain awareness in the present moment when distress is present, because truly experiencing the present as it is means we have to refrain from our most habitual defenses, such as justifying, trying to get control, going numb, seeking diversions, and so on. The sole purpose of these strategies is to protect us from feeling the discomfort that we don't want to feel. But until we can refrain from these defenses and feel the physical experience directly, we will stay stuck in the story line of "Me," and remain unaware of what life really is in the moment.

For example, if we're anxious, it's natural to want to avoid feeling it. We may stay busy to occupy ourselves, or try harder, or try to figure things out in ways that are not necessary or practical, such as rehashing our childhood. But if we can ask ourselves "What is this?" the only important and real answer comes from the actual physical experience of anxiety in the present moment. Remember, we're not asking what it's *about*, which is analyzing—and the opposite of being physically present. We're simply asking what it actually is.

Asking the question, "What is this?" is the essence of awakening the quality of curiosity, in that the only "answer" comes from being open to actually experiencing the reality of each moment. Curiosity means that we're willing to explore unknown territory—the places the ego doesn't want to go. Curiosity allows us to take a step at our edge, toward our deepest fears. Being truly curious means we're willing to say yes to our experience, even the hard parts, instead of indulging the no of our habitual resistance.

Saying yes doesn't mean we like our experience or that we necessarily feel accepting. It doesn't even mean that we override the no. Saying yes simply means that we pay attention—meticulous attention—to the no. It means we're no longer resisting the people, things, and fears we don't like; instead we're learning to open to them, to invite them in, to welcome them with curiosity in order to experience what's actually going on.

Yet sometimes, when the mind is reeling in the panic of self-doubt and confusion, it is particularly difficult to come back to the heart that seeks to awaken. In these moments, how can we find the willingness to stay present with our own fears—the fears that will always limit our ability to love? When everything seems dark and unworkable, when we've even lost touch with the desire to move toward the light, the one thing we can do is take a deep breath into the center of the chest on the in-breath, and on the out-breath we can extend to ourselves the same warmth and compassion that we would offer to a friend or child in distress. Breathing into the heart, physically connecting with the center of our being, is a way to extend kindness to ourselves even when there appears to be no kindness in sight.

While remembering that our distress is also our path, and breathing the distressing sensations into the center of the chest— we can learn to stay with the actual unwanted sensations. It's important to understand that being able to ask "What is this?"— and truly reside with what we find there—takes a great deal of patience and courage. Maybe we can only do it a little. But we persevere—even if it's just three breaths at a time. Ultimately, it's awareness that heals. It's awareness that allows us to reconnect with the heart, the heart that is the essence of our being.

Recently I was told that I had to have a particularly unpleasant medical procedure. Combined with the fear around the thought of having the procedure were the memories of painful experiences of prior similar medical procedures, leading to a feeling of dread and morbidity. Over the years I've become free from many of my fears and attachments, but each of us has our own particular edge—that place beyond which fear tells us not to go—so even though I had extensive experience practicing with illness and pain, there was no doubt that this particular set of circumstances put me at my personal edge.

It was helpful to ask the first question—"What is going on right now?"—because that enabled me to see that there was actually no physical discomfort other than the discomfort triggered by believing my fear-based thoughts. It was also helpful to ask, "Can I see this situation as my path?"—pointing to the opportunity to work with my own particular attachments and fears. As well, asking, "What are my most believed thoughts?" allowed me to see that thoughts such as "This is too much" and "I can't do this" were just thoughts—thoughts that were not the truth, no matter how accurate they felt in the moment.

But the real key to working with the panic and dread came from answering the question, "What is this?" Beyond the thoughts, what is it that experiences? The answer was to come back again and again to the physical experience of the present moment, such as the sensations of tightness in the chest and queasiness in the stomach. Sometimes I could only stay with it for the duration of three breaths. Sometimes the experience was so strong all I could do was breathe the sensations into the center of the chest while remembering all those others who were suffering from the same or similar distress and wishing compassion to all of us.

Staying with the "What is this?" question eventually allowed the self-imposed prison wall of fear to begin to dissolve, and I was able to experience the grace and freedom of surrender. When we can viscerally enter into the question "What is this?" we will see that our experience of "Me-ness," of being a small-minded separate self, however unpleasant, is constantly changing, and that at bottom, it is just a combination of believed thoughts, physical sensations, and old memories. We realize that the small mind—the mind of "I-as-a-Me"—is not who we truly are. Once we see this, the experience of distress begins to unravel into its individual aggregates rather than seeming so solid. Again, it's awareness that heals.

5. "Can I Let This Experience Just Be?"

This is not easy to do, because our human compulsion toward comfort drives us to want to fix or get rid of our unpleasant experiences. To allow our experience to just be usually becomes possible only after we've become disappointed by the futility of trying to fix ourselves (and others). We have to realize that trying to change or let go of the feelings we don't want to feel simply doesn't work. Allowing our experience to just be requires a critical understanding: that it's more painful to try to push away our own pain than it is to feel it. This understanding is not intellectual; it's something that eventually takes root in the core of our being.

Once we can really let our experience be as it is, awareness becomes a more spacious container, within which distress begins to dismantle on its own. Sometimes it helps to widen the container by intentionally including the awareness of air and sounds, or whatever we can connect with that is outside the skin boundary. Within this wider and more spacious container, the distress may even transform from something heavy and somber into pure, nondescript energy, which is more porous and light. The energy may then release on its own, without any need to try to get rid of it.

This final question—"Can I let this experience just be?"— also allows the quality of mercy or loving-kindness to come forth, because we're no longer judging ourselves or our experience as defective. We're finally willing to experience our life within the spaciousness of the heart, rather than through the self-limiting judgments of the mind.

These five questions—"What is going on right now?" "Can I welcome this as my path?" "What is my most believed thought?" "What is this?" and "Can I let this experience just be?"— remind us of the key steps needed to work with our emotional distress. Some students carry little laminated cards with the five questions in their pockets for times when cognitive shock takes hold, when everything we know is temporarily forgotten. Each time we remember to ask one of these questions, it is like opening a doorway into reality, and we are back on the path of learning to live more authentically.

Remember, though, these questions are just pointers; it's important not to get lost in the technique. From a broader perspective, the reason we ask these questions is that when we have emotional distress, we are usually caught in our small mind, in own self-imposed prison walls—of anger, fear, and confusion. But when our self-imposed prison walls come down, all that remains is the connectedness that we are.

5

Transforming Energy

E veryone is familiar with the state of being too busy—going, going, going, and doing, doing, doing. The usual result: stressing, stressing, stressing. There's a physical feeling of scattered energy, and even if we sit down to meditate, instead of feeling inwardly settled, we may still feel scattered, with no sense of center or direction. This is why it's so crucial to develop the ability to focus—to rein in and transform the scattered energy into a sense of inner strength and settledness. There's a specific meditation practice that is particularly beneficial in bringing our energy into a more concentrated focus. It's called "*hara* practice" because it pertains to the area right below the belly button that is commonly called the hara, both in Zen and in the martial arts. This particular area is also recognized in acupuncture as a center of strength and energy.

My initial meditation training included the cultivation of the hara through concentrated breathing practices. Over the many years that I did a focused hara practice I had a lot of interesting experiences. Once, after my very first five-day meditation retreat, after focusing intensely on the hara, it felt like I actually had tentacles of energy coming out of my belly. The day after the retreat I was going to a dawn meditation, at a rural property where you had to go down a steep, rocky path to get to the meditation room. It was totally dark out, but on that morning I was able to run down the path without looking, feeling as if tentacles of energy were guiding me. Don't get the wrong idea—I never had this experience again. It was a onetime free ride. In fact, by the next day the effects of the retreat had mostly worn off. The point is, although having special states of mind is not what spiritual practice is about, it's nonetheless possible to transform our normal scattered energy into a very focused form of concentration. Over time this can develop into a sense of inner strength, and also into a resolve to stay present that carries over into our everyday life activities.

Much of what we know about hara practice comes from traditional Japanese Zen, which originally was closely aligned with the samurai culture. Far from promoting the traditional Buddhist flavor of reverence for life, specific breathing and concentration techniques were taught that centered on strengthening the hara, so that the samurai could shut out all distractions and learn to bear pain and even death with indifference. Although Zen is no longer practiced in this stoic, militaristic way, there is no doubt that the hara—through breathing and special exercises—can be strengthened to the point where it is a source of physical and mental power.

Hara practice is a focused concentration exercise designed to consolidate the scattered energy in the body, as well as the energy that we take in on the inhale, into an inner strength in the area of the belly (hara). The instructions are quite simple: On the in-breath you bring awareness to the belly. The inhale is intentional—long and slow—as you feel the belly fill up. The out-breath is also slow and long. If it's helpful, you can visualize or sense the belly as a bed of hot coals, and with each in-breath the coals turn red-hot, as if a bellows were fanning a fire. On the out-breath, you breathe consciously through the back of the throat and the nose, making the very slight but inaudible humming sound of *huuuum*. Try this—it probably won't feel at all unusual. On the out-breath, visualize or sense the coals staying red-hot. If this is difficult to visualize, it's fine to simply feel the sense of warmth. As the coals get hotter, and as you make the particular sound of *huuuum,* you can feel the energy and strength consolidate in the hara.

Hara practice serves as a foundation—it strengthens the ability to focus, without which we couldn't stay present, especially when distractions are strong. Yet it's important to understand that hara practice is not a complete practice in itself, primarily because it shuts' life out. In fact, when thoughts or emotional reactions come up during the hara meditation, the instruction is to put the thoughts and reactions to the side and return to a focused attention on the breath into the hara. This is the one-pointedness of unwavering attention: keeping the focus solely on the breath as it moves in and out of the belly. This is both the strength and the limitation of hara practice, since it doesn't deal with the whole spectrum of our mental and emotional life. But even though it's not a complete practice, it's still a very valuable one.

When doing a hara practice, the biggest barrier is the sometimes unrelenting spinning of the mind, when it insists on staying caught in stories—about what happened, what might happen, about our plans and fantasies, and sometimes stories about things we don't even care about. Intrinsic to all of these stories is a particular quality of energy—the scattered energy of the spinning mind. What makes the hara practice so valuable is that it can harness and transform this scattered energy, leaving the mind much more calm and stable, thus allowing us to actually live our life with more clarity and awareness. However, the only way for this meditation to be effective is if we can muster the firm resolve not to get pulled into thinking. We may even have to tell ourselves, "Don't go there!" when compelling thoughts arise. But the benefits will become obvious within a reasonable time.

THREE-BY-THREE

Here are the specific instructions for a guided hara meditation so that you can get an experiential feel for how to do it. It is useful to do a five-minute warm-up meditation, called a "Three-by-Three," to initiate the process of harnessing the scattered energy. In a Three-by-Three you bring awareness to three different aspects of awareness and hold them in focus for three full breaths. For example, you could be simultaneously aware of the breath, your hands, and the perception of sounds for the duration of three full breaths. Here's a brief guided run-through.

Round One

Start with awareness of the breath in and out of the nose, feeling the coolness on the in-breath and the subtle texture on the out-breath. Stay with these physical sensations for three breaths.

Now, while staying aware of the physical sensations of the breath in and out of the nose, add awareness of your hands resting in your lap. Feel the actual physical feelings in your hands, and stay with awareness of breath and hands for three breaths.

Finally, while staying aware of the breath and your hands, become aware of any sounds and try to maintain awareness of all three components for three full breaths. If you can't stay present with all three simultaneously, it's okay to quickly flip back and forth between them.

Round Two

Take a couple of deeper breaths to clear the mind, then bring awareness again to the breath, this time focusing on the physical sensations in the chest. Feel the expansion and contraction of your upper body as the breath goes in and out, and stay with these sensations for three breaths.

Continue to be aware of the breath while adding awareness of your buttocks, sitting on the cushion or chair. Feel the sensations of touch and pressure, and stay with the breath and awareness of the buttocks for three breaths.

Last, while staying aware of the breath and your buttocks, add awareness of the quality of light in the room, and stay with all three of these as best you can for three full breaths.

Round Three

Again take a couple of deeper breaths, then bring awareness to the breath in the area of the belly. Feel the physical sensations in the belly area as you breathe in and out, and stay with these sensations for three breaths.

Now add awareness of the physical experience in the area of your shoulders. Feel any tension or feelings that reside there, and stay with these sensations along with the breath in the belly for three breaths.

Last, while staying with the breath and the shoulders, add the perception of the sense of space in the room, and stay with these three things for three full breaths.

You can change the individual components of the Three-by-Three as you wish; I usually use feeling the breath in one particular area of the body, such as the nose or the belly; one physical sensation in the body; and one area outside the body, such as sounds or light. The important point is to really focus on whatever you choose and to try to harness the energy by refraining from letting thinking take over. At first it may be difficult to do the Three-by-Threes; but it's like exercising a muscle— the more we do it, the stronger our ability to sustain awareness becomes.

As you conclude the last round of the Three-by-Three, you move directly into the hara meditation.

Hara Meditation

On the in-breath bring awareness to the belly. The tongue should be resting on the upper palate. You can place your hands over the area right below the belly button.

The eyes can be open, but looking downward and unfocused, or closed.

The in-breath should be long and slow as you feel the belly fill up. The out-breath is also long and slow.

Visualize or sense the belly as a bed of hot coals, and with each in-breath the coals turn red-hot, as if a bellows is blowing on a fire.

On the out-breath, breathe consciously through the back of the throat and nose, making the very slight inaudible humming sound of *huuuum*.

Visualize or sense the coals staying red-hot on the outbreath.

If it is difficult to visualize the coals getting hot, it's fine to simply feel their warmth.

As the coals get hotter, feel the energy and strength consolidate in the hara.

Do this for several breaths.

If thoughts arise—turn away—there's no need to pay any attention to them.

If emotions arise—again, refrain from feeling or exploring them.

Remember: energy follows attention. If you put your attention in the belly, the energy will follow. But you don't have to push or strain.

Just feel the belly filling up. Feel the energy there. Keep the attention there.

Remember to make the sound of *huuuum* on the out-breath.

This is important—there should be no gap in awareness of the belly between the end of the out-breath and the beginning of the in-breath. Likewise, there should be no gap in awareness between the end of the in-breath and the beginning of the out-breath—just total, continuous absorption on the area of the hara.

Stay with awareness of the breath in and out of the belly. Feel the belly expanding. Feel the heat, the energy, the strength.

For an optional final step: on the out-breath visualize or sense the energy from the coals going to the whole middle area of the body, and perhaps even beyond. Do this for several breaths. Feel the body filling up with strength.

If you are interested, you can experiment with this, including doing it when you first begin a meditation and then moving into a more open awareness after ten to twenty minutes. You may find that the focused concentration of the hara practice is the natural foundation for a more open awareness practice. You can also do it for a few breaths at a time, anytime throughout the day.

I've found the hara practice to be one of the most effective tools for staying focused, and if you have never really developed a focused concentration practice, the hara meditation would be a good way to work on it. You might even find that spending fifteen to twenty minutes not allowing the mind to spin results in a settling down in both body and mind, with the resultant state of genuine tranquillity.

One other suggestion for when the attention wanders, which it surely will: Come back to the very specifics of the technique, such as the lengthening and slowing of the breath, or visualizing the hot coals, or most importantly, to the sound of the breath on the exhale. I've found that this allows me to go right back into a focused awareness. Remember, you're not expected to do this well at first, so don't set up unrealistic expectations, which will just lead to disappointment and self-judgment. This technique requires effort and practice—"practice" in the traditional sense, such as practicing playing the piano. And as with any endeavor that requires effort and practice, strength exercised equals more strength; weakness indulged equals more weakness.

Transforming the Energy of Anger

There is another particular situation where working with the hara can be very useful, and that's when we have the strong energy of anger. When anger arises, it has two components: one, the sensations and energy in the body; and two, the thoughts that are often racing through the mind, such as "He's such a jerk," or "I hate this," or "This isn't fair." What is required to transform the energy of anger from a strong negative force into something potentially beneficial is to first be able to refrain from letting the thoughts run rampant.

The practice is to repeatedly turn away from the thoughts, because each time we entertain them, it is like throwing a log on a fire, fueling the negative energy. To help us turn away from the thoughts, we bring the attention again and again to the breath in the belly. We stay focused like a laser on the hara, and come back to it each time we get pulled back into thinking, blaming, or self-justifying.

Then, to actually transform the negative energy of anger, we feel the sensations and particularly the energy of anger as it flows through the body, and on the in-breath we breathe *as if* we were breathing that energy directly into the hara. If you can do this for several breaths, remembering to make the *huuuum* sound on the out-breath, you will begin to feel a definite change in your body energy—the strong feeling of negativity being transformed into a definitive sense of strength and resolve, which can then be channeled in a positive direction. This process is hard to describe, but it's definitely worth experimenting with.

Transforming Sexual Energy

Equally hard to describe is how we can transform our sexual energy into a sense of inner strength. This is particularly valuable when we are caught in strong sexual fantasies or desires. Just like working with the negative energy of anger, we have to first be able to turn away from indulging the specific thoughts and images. This is where bringing a focused attention to the hara can be helpful.

As we settle into the hara—and this may well be a back-and-forth struggle, as the small mind wants to indulge the fantasies and desires—we then bring awareness to the specific experience of the sexual energy itself as it flows through the body. And on the in-breath we breath *as if* we were breathing that energy directly into the hara; then on the out-breath we allow the experience to consolidate with the *huuuum* sound. Sometimes all it takes is several very focused breaths—as we breathe the energy into the belly area—before the energy subsides and begins to transform into a definitive feeling of strength in the hara. We can in turn use that strength to be more fully present, or we can channel it into productive activity.

As with the transformation of the negative energy of anger, transforming our sexual energy is worth the experiment. When we indulge either of these, we're leaking away valuable energy— energy that we could use to further awareness and spiritual growth. Note: this isn't saying that sex is bad—it's the fantasies that aren't helpful. Conversely, when we harness and transform the energy through bringing it into the hara, it becomes possible to channel that energy in a positive direction.

In working with the hara it is good to keep in mind that all practices have built-in detours—that is, ways in which we can misuse the practice and move away from our intended direction. The hara practice tends to produce states of inner stillness and calm (as we get out of the spinning mind), and this can be quite seductive. We can forget that the practice is a limited one, in that we are purposely shutting much of life out. This can possibly lead to "spiritual bypass," where we end up ignoring the things inside that we don't want to face—the exact things that keep us from experiencing freedom, such as our unhealthy patterns and deepest fears. That said, it's also true that hara practice doesn't have to lead to the detour of spiritual bypass. It can instead be a valuable tool in developing both concentration and a kind of inner strength that is invaluable in itself. Hara practice allows us to know ourselves, to know our body—and to understand what is required to transform the energy in the body into something that serves us on the path to living authentically.

PART TWO

Awakening the Mind

6

What about Happiness?

Does living the authentic life mean that we'll be happy? This is a valid question, because many people believe that the purpose of human life is to be happy. For centuries teachers have offered prescriptions for happiness, and in the last few decades there have been increasing promises of quick fixes—guarantees to take away our anxiety and depression and replace them with a cheerful outlook. But evidence suggests that in recent years our levels of anxiety have actually increased, and what we thought we knew about how to be happy is now open to question; so perhaps we should ask first, what do we mean by happiness?

A while back a student told me he really didn't care about being enlightened or anything deeply spiritual—he said he just wanted to be happy. He asked me if, after my years of meditating, I felt I was truly happy. I told him that yes, I could say I was happy, but perhaps my understanding of what it meant to be happy was different from how he might understand it. Again, the question is, what does it mean to be happy?

PERSONAL HAPPINESS

The dictionary describes happiness as a state characterized by delight or contentment—the emotional feeling that life is good. It is almost always associated with getting the good stuff, such as pleasure, or getting the things we want, such as satisfying relationships, financial security, or good health. When people talk about happiness, they are usually referring to this version of everyday personal happiness. It's important to realize that all of these aspects of happiness are based, in part, on our external life circumstances. But externals can always change—we can lose our job, or our wealth, or our relationships, or our health. Eventually we have to accept that relying on externals is not a very sound foundation for true contentment.

It may take us many years and many disappointments to realize the fact that we can't rely on externals for happiness. But if externals are not the source of happiness, where else can we turn? How about spiritual practice—can it actually make us happier? There's a study in which participants were asked to listen to a piece of classical music. Half were told to try to feel happy while listening to the music; the other half were told to just listen. Interestingly, the participants who were trying to be happy reported being much less so than those who were just listening. Why? Because in *trying* to be happy they were caught in their heads, in their small minds, whereas simply being present with the music allowed the other participants to experience the genuine happiness of just being here, not trying to feel different. It's becoming increasingly clear that people who practice meditation and who try to live in a way that is more present and more awake, generally experience increasing happiness in life.

Yet, in spiritual practice, happiness is not the goal. If we make happiness the goal, it will most likely elude us, as it did with the people trying to feel happy while listening to music. Happiness is not so much a good feeling that we can capture as it is a by-product of how we live and how we see life. This leads back to the question, what do we actually mean by happiness? It's important to understand that personal happiness is based on a myth, which tells us that we'll be happy if we get what we want—the right mate, the right job, the right body, and so on. These things may be enjoyable in the very short term, but happiness based on externals will rarely survive life's inevitable blows.

It's also a myth that we can't be happy if we get what we *don't* want, namely discomfort in any form. Yet as many who have suffered through serious difficulties have learned, it is possible to experience genuine equanimity even in the midst of prolonged discomfort. As long as we believe in these myths, and keep trying to attain happiness by controlling our behaviors—whether through trying to please others, trying harder to succeed, or seeking comfort and diversions—we will continue to trap ourselves in the up-and-down cycle of personal happiness and unhappiness.

Genuine Happiness

There is another kind of happiness that goes beyond personal happiness. I've written extensively about it in my book *Beyond Happiness* (Shambhala Publications, 2010). Essentially, this is the deeper, more genuine experience of true contentment—of being fundamentally at ease with life as it is. The basic teaching underlying every religion and every spiritual path is that it's possible to experience this fundamental happiness, where we're no longer attached to our demand that life be a particular way. But it's important to understand that this happiness has to come from within; it cannot depend on external life circumstances or on good emotional feelings.

In meditation practice, whenever we strive for special experiences to bring us happiness, we are caught in the grasping of the small mind, in the self-centered pursuit of wanting to feel a particular way. This is spiritual materialism, and it is guaranteed to undermine our more genuine quest to realize our true nature, which is ultimately the source of the deeper equanimity of genuine happiness. We may easily get sidetracked from this quest with promises or easy formulas to bring us happiness—even spiritual-sounding ones, such as seeking after enlightenment experiences. However, formulas for happiness give us only superficial fixes; they don't and can't go to the root.

In short, happiness doesn't come from making happiness the goal—it comes from being able to appreciate the journey, particularly the present-moment experience of our life. To "enjoy the ride" doesn't mean we're going to get somewhere, have a fun time, or get something—it means we're curious about what our life is, and willing to actually live our life as it is, and even appreciate it—including the most difficult, unpleasant, unwanted aspects of it.

In this sense, we can say that true happiness is more about being present, being awake, being open, than it is about being happy in the feel-good Hollywood sense of being merry and cheerful. Genuine happiness is not exhilaration; nor is it about being upbeat all the time. These may come and go, but genuine happiness at its core includes the willingness to acknowledge the painful aspects of life right alongside all the parts we normally deem as "good" or "happy."

WHAT BLOCKS HAPPINESS?

Instead of trying to stamp out our unwanted feelings and behaviors, the path to true happiness requires our openhearted attention to the exact things that seem to block our way to it—especially to the things we want to run away from, change, or get rid of. Thus, when we're feeling unhappy, rather than trying to generate happiness, we must try instead to see that *whatever* is on our plate is our opportunity, our path.

In other words, learning to live from genuine happiness requires first seeing what blocks it. One of the major blocks is our deep-rooted sense of entitlement. In fact, a big part of the "happiness problem" is that we firmly believe that we *should* be happy. We think it's our right and consequently we feel entitled to it. Our sense of entitlement tells us that life should go the way we want and expect it to go; it even tells us we shouldn't have to experience any discomfort. The result: When discomfort arises, we feel that something is wrong. Then we might get angry or feel it's unfair or feel sorry for ourselves.

Along with our sense of entitlement, we have many specific ideas and expectations about what will make us feel happy. "If only I had the right partner, I'd be happy." "If only I had more money or a better job, I'd no longer be anxious." "If only I had a better body, I'd be content." "If only I had an enlightenment experience, then I would be at peace." All of our "if onlies" are aspects of a basic unwillingness to actually be with the life that we have at the moment. Instead, we choose to live in hopeful fantasies about the future. This is certainly understandable, in that we'd rather picture a different and better reality than be with what life actually presents. Yet where does this leave us? It leaves us living a life that is neither real nor satisfying.

Another major block to genuine happiness is being caught in the thinking mind—lamenting about the past or worrying about the future. Living in our heads, we nurture the small mind of self-centeredness—the ground of all our judgments, fears, and limiting beliefs—and it literally guarantees our unhappiness. This keeps us caught in our emotions, particularly anger, fear, and despair, which cut us off from living from our true openhearted nature. Anger, for example, is rooted in aversion to life, and it separates us from others.

Paradoxically, even though these separating emotions are a prescription for unhappiness, we often don't want to give them up. In our misguided quest for personal happiness (in contrast to deeper or more genuine happiness), we believe that these emotions will somehow serve us. For example, in spite of all the evidence to the contrary, we continue to believe that anger will help protect us and empower us in getting what we want. We also love being right, because we like the juiciness and the false sense of power that accompanies our self-righteousness. Unfortunately, we would often rather feel right than be happy. But like all of the disconnecting emotions, this leaves us with the unsatisfying feeling of being separate—which guarantees unhappiness.

Interestingly, even if we are not caught in our emotions or not feeling particularly unhappy, we may still not experience genuine happiness. In other words, we can be gliding along through life with good health, a decent job, and satisfactory relationships, but still be far from experiencing the deeper sense of equanimity and appreciation that are the result of living more authentically. When we're caught up in the complacency of our routines, living our life on autopilot, we may be somewhat buffered from being actively unhappy. Yet we're still skating on thin ice. Sooner or later, however, the anxious quiver in our being will come to the surface, and we may feel the ache of the emptiness of our pursuits or the nagging feeling that something is missing.

WHY WE STAY STUCK

The real question we need to ask ourselves is, "Why do we continue to follow behaviors that don't bring us real happiness?" The answer lies in the basic human condition: We are born with the survival instinct for safety, security, and control; we are also born with an aversion to discomfort and a natural desire for comfort and pleasure. These basic human predispositions are bound to dictate our behaviors, as we can clearly see by looking at two-year-olds. Although there's nothing wrong with trying to be safe or comfortable, the problem is one of priorities: when our survival mode is prioritized, our other natural urges— curiosity, appreciation, and living from our true openhearted nature—are pushed aside. Consequently, we live increasingly from our small self, believing that our survival-based behavior strategies of trying harder or people-pleasing will make us happy. Yet ironically, these very behaviors, along with our many addictive behaviors, starting with our addictions to pleasure and diversions, often bring us the most dissatisfaction.

In themselves, pleasure and diversions are fine, and they can certainly make us feel good. But pursuing our addictive behaviors is the very essence of the human tendency to misunderstand happiness. We follow these seductive behaviors because they seem to promise us happiness. And to some degree, they fulfill their promise in that we feel happy when we experience sensual pleasure or the hit of endorphins. But the fulfillment of that promise is always temporary, and it is always based on a temporarily benevolent external environment. As long as the environment doesn't turn against us, we think our life is okay, and we don't do anything to change the situation. Nor do we address the underlying unease out of which the addictive behaviors arise. After all, why upset the applecart when things seem to be okay? We may glide along, feeling good for a time, but because we haven't addressed that hole of neediness inside, we will feel the compulsion to cover it over with pleasure or diversions again and again. Thus, we remain on the treadmill of personal happiness/unhappiness. When we don't feel so good, we find a fix, and feel temporarily happy. As the cycle goes on and on, the genuine happiness of living authentically eludes us.

Wherever we find ourselves stuck, whether it's in our entitlements, if-onlies, emotions, or addictive behaviors—if we aspire to live authentically, we have to look honestly at how we're avoiding reality, how we let our life slip by while ignoring the things we know we will eventually have to face. Living authentically requires that we be present with our life exactly as it is. We can ask ourselves the question, "What is this?" and use this question to focus like a laser on our present-moment experience. This is the *only* place we can practice: in exactly what we are experiencing right now. The courage to be honest with ourselves and to not turn away is well worth the effort. Resting in the physical experience of the present moment, including the places where we're most stuck, the apparent solidity of those stuck places gradually becomes more and more porous.

THE GENEROSITY OF THE HEART

Along with the continuing effort to be present, working with what gets in the way of genuine happiness eventually uncovers one of its major roots: living mainly to get something for ourselves. The alternative is to give from the natural generosity of the heart. When we truly offer ourselves to someone in need—whether they are hurting or deprived in some way—we experience the gratitude of living from the awakened heart, and we feel the fulfillment of acting from a sense of our basic connectedness.

Paradoxically, even though we know we are happier when we do these things, research shows that when we're given the choice between doing something self-serving and doing something altruistic, more often than not we will choose the self-centered alternative. Sadly, as this research shows, we often don't do what makes us genuinely happy. We may have to be repeatedly disappointed by living a self-centered life before our desire for the happiness of others is awakened. But once it is awakened, living from this natural generosity allows us to move from our small mind of separateness to cultivating this essential root of true contentment.

There are many different ways to give. We can volunteer or give through social action, and we can certainly learn to give in small ways throughout the day. For example, giving can be as simple as letting someone get in front of you in line or doing the dishes because you see that your partner or roommate is tired. Or perhaps it might involve really listening to a friend who is hurting and in need of connection. In short, one of the real keys to living most genuinely is to give oneself to others, without personal agendas. When we're truly generous, we give to others without ulterior motives or a sense of self-importance. In other words, we're not drawing attention to ourselves, and our giving isn't just another way of propping up our self-image or a way of trying to get appreciation. Nor are we motivated by the idea that we *should* be more giving.

If we reflect on what it means to give from the natural generosity of the heart, at some point it becomes clear that giving may first mean *giving up:* giving up our strong identification with being only our small, separate self. This is the self of judgments and fears, the self that holds back from the natural inclination to give, either through laziness or a sense of entitlement or self-doubt. As our identification with our small self recedes and we become increasingly present, we gradually discover who we truly are—our natural being of connectedness and love.

We can then understand that the purpose of human life is not to be happy, although we certainly all want that. The purpose of human life is to awaken to our true self. The more we are in touch with our true self, the closer we are to living from genuine happiness. Although there is no "secret" to living a genuinely happy life, the deepest happiness of equanimity and connectedness grows with our ability to stay present with life as it is. And this flowers as we water the roots of the generosity of the heart—including our inherent capacity for gratitude, lovingkindness, and compassion. This is how we learn to live from the connectedness that we are. This is also the essence of what it means to live the authentic life.

7

No One Special to Be

One of the main characteristics of a life of sleep is that we are totally identified with being a "Me." Starting with our name, our history, our self-images and identities, we use each one of these things to solidify the sense that we are living in our little subjective sphere. We experience ourselves as "special"—not in the normal sense of being distinguished or exceptional, but in the sense that we feel unique and subtly significant. Interestingly, our feeling of specialness is not just from having positive qualities; we can even use our suffering to make us feel unique and special. Yet not *needing* to be special, not needing to be *any* particular way, is what it means to be free—free to experience our natural being, our most authentic self.

For example, we all have images of ourselves that we unconsciously carry with us throughout our waking hours. Our self-images are the conceptions or pictures of how we see ourselves. We can have the self-image of being nice, or competent, or deep; or we could have a negative self-image—seeing ourselves as weak, or stupid, or worthless. Usually we try to focus on our positive self-images, and we often try to shape our external life to portray ourselves in the most favorable way. We live out of the vanity of trying to look a particular way, mostly to gain the approval of those whose opinion is most important to us. Whether it's our clothes, our hair, our body—our radar for approval is constantly running, mostly unconsciously. This is true even with the car we drive; whether it's a Cadillac or a hybrid or a pick-up truck, when we sit behind the wheel, it defines who we are to ourselves and to others, and we are usually totally identified with that image.

Much of our life is spent trying to live out of our self-images, and we rarely have the inclination to look at them honestly. In fact, it is very difficult to be truly honest with ourselves, especially since we can simultaneously have both positive and negative self-images on board and may not recognize their inconsistency. This is due to the fact that we all wear blinders—a psychological defense that doesn't allow one part of ourselves to see another part. For example, if we need to see ourselves as nice, we may ignore all of our harmful or self-centered qualities. Or, if we need to see ourselves as unworthy, we'll ignore all the positive data. This is actually quite common.

Closely related to our self-images are our identities—how we define ourselves according to the roles we play, such as mother, businessman, meditator, athlete, and so on. The identities we assume don't have to make sense. For example, even though I've written five books and many published essays, I still don't have the identity of being a writer. And stranger still, even though I've been severely limited in my physical activities for over twenty years due to a chronic immune system condition, I still see myself as an athlete. Actually it doesn't really matter if our identities make sense; what matters is how attached to them we are in our need to define ourselves.

Both our self-images and our identities become part and parcel of the stories we weave about ourselves. Almost always these stories are skewered versions of the truth concerning who we are—our history, our victimhood, why we're angry, and on and on. We are caught in a story when we tell ourselves, "I'm worthless," or "I'm depressed," or "People should appreciate me." We're particularly caught when we say, "I'm this way because . . . ," and then assign blame to others such as our parents or to something that happened to us. We can also know we're wrapped up in one of our many stories if we have the thought "I'm the kind of person who . . . ," or "I'm not the kind of person who . . . ." For example, "I'm the kind of person who has to be alone." Or, "I'm not the kind of person who can be disciplined." The point is, most of our stories are self-deceptions in that they are partially manufactured versions of the truth—truths we adopt in order to feel a particular way. But living out of stories prevents us from living more genuinely.

Another universal version of living out of stories is holding on to our beliefs, many of which are illusions. For example, most of us have the belief, the illusion, that we are in control, or that we *can* be in control. We cling to this illusion because the fear of loss of control is one of our strongest fears. Even when we see all the evidence to the contrary, we still live our day-to-day life with the illusion that we're in the driver's seat. In fact, many of our personality strategies are based on this illusion. For instance, we think that following the control strategy of trying to please others will keep us safe from disapproval. Or we might think if we follow the control strategy of trying harder, we can make life go as we would like. The point is, each closely held belief, such as the illusion of control, defines us and limits us in many ways we can't even see.

Another universal illusion, or story, is the belief that what we "know" is The Truth. We believe our thoughts and our opinions, usually without ever questioning them, forgetting that they are all relative, flawed, and limited. When we have an opinion about someone or something, we're rarely aware that it's just an opinion. The illusion—or self-deception—is that what we're believing is The Truth. Yet in spite of the basic insanity of believing our thoughts, we do it all the time. We firmly believe what we want to believe—we often won't even entertain other possibilities. In light of the fact that we can deceive ourselves about almost anything, honest self-observation is often a study in living free from illusions, particularly the illusions that narrowly dictate how we live our lives.

Perhaps the most pivotal story we tell ourselves is the deep-seated illusion that we are one single, permanent self. Yet simple observation would show us that we are really a collection of many "Me's," or personas. Which "Me" predominates depends on which self-image or identity we're believing in, and also on what beliefs we're holding to in the moment. A simple example is how the mood we're in determines how we see things—if we're in a good mood, other people may seem fine to us, whereas if our mood turns sour, the exact same people may seem to be irritating. Or a more telling example: We can see ourselves as trustworthy and upright, and firmly pledge that we won't engage in a particular behavior again, such as drinking or overeating. But two hours later we may find ourselves doing the exact thing we sincerely believed we wouldn't do. Often these Me's are not even in touch with one another, which is another example of our psychological blinders that don't allow one part to see another part.

Given that we have examples of similar situations every day, how can we continue to believe in the story of being a single, unchanging self? In fact, the whole notion that who we are is limited to the story of a single self is perhaps the main illusion that spiritual practice addresses. This is why one of the deepest teachings is that there is no one special that we need to be. In other words, to be inwardly free means we don't have to live out of our self-images and identities; we don't have to feel a particular way; we don't have to believe the stories we tell ourselves—the stories that dictate who we are and how we live.

In order to experience the freedom of living a more authentic life, it is absolutely necessary that we drop our stories and illusions. This is certainly not easy to do, and it helps to know what it actually looks like to live authentically. First and foremost, living authentically means living with honesty—being willing to look at our own illusions and self-deceptions; questioning our self-images and self-limiting identities; examining the stories we weave about ourselves, including our stories about our past and who we are. Many of our convictions, ideals, and "shoulds" are just mental constructs, born out of our conditioning. Do we have the courage to see them for what they are? Can we experience the freedom of no longer using them as a prop?

We have to realize how our identities, convictions, and stories prop up our sense of purpose and importance in order to subtly make us feel special. We count on these props to give us a feeling of solidity and security. When we lose one of these props, such as when losing our job or having a relationship failure, we naturally experience anxiety: without our familiar supports we are left with just ourselves, which is a frightening prospect. This is why we try to fill our lives with busyness and doing, as well as with our many diversions and entertainments—to guarantee that we are never left alone with ourselves. We don't want to feel that hole of emptiness. Some people even experience this when they have no plans for the day. Upon awakening, instead of looking forward to a free day of relaxation, there's a feeling of being lost: "Who will I be? What will I do?" This means that the ability to be truly at home with oneself hasn't been cultivated.

But as we see through our illusions, identities, and stories, they decreasingly dictate how we feel and how we live. This is what it means, in part, to live authentically—no longer fooling ourselves with our illusions and self-deceptions. But in order to be free of them, we first have to *see* them with both clarity and precision. What this requires more than anything is being open to our life—being willing to face the things we've never wanted to face. This includes our fears—of rejection, unworthiness, and uncertainty. To be open, to be present, in turn allows us the possibility of no longer sleepwalking through life, just seeking comfort, security, and approval, and no longer living with the illusion that we have endless time.

In aspiring to live more authentically it's important that we don't set up unrealistic ideals—the ideal that we should always be present, or be able to drop all of our self-images, or never indulge ourselves in diversions. That would be a simplistic moral stance. A much healthier stance is that we at least need to *have the intention* to live more honestly and more awake. And also with more kindness toward ourselves for the many times we will falter, including when we don't look at ourselves with honesty, or when we waste time instead of meditating, or holler at somebody just because we're in a bad mood. Feeling guilty when these things inevitably happen is unnecessary and not at all helpful. What is helpful, however, is to occasionally feel remorse for not living from our true heart, from our aspiration to live more awake.

On the long path of practice we move from living from our self-images and our many stories to living more from our deepest values, our most authentic self. When I reflect on the teachers

I have most admired, the values that stand out the most are: honesty in looking at one's life, not settling for complacency, living with presence, inner quiet, and inner strength, and living with appreciation and kindness—all of which contribute to true contentment. What gets in the way of this movement toward our authentic self, more than anything, is our insistence on identifying with the small self—preserving our narrow world of being special, of needing to look and feel a particular way. When we are faced with a choice point, we can remember the question of the eternal recurrence. In order to turn away from the small self and toward what is most genuine, we ask ourselves, "If I were to live this life over again an eternal number of times in the exact same way, what would I do in this situation?" Reflecting with honesty on what is our true path, on what we most value, we can take the step to avoid the inauthentic, to avoid the remorse of living dishonestly.

Sometimes this step will require courage, to break free of the complacency of the familiar. One student described to me how she was very caught in her vanity, to the point where she thought constantly about what she would wear and how she would look. I suggested she devote one day a week to having a "bad-hair day," where she would consciously and purposefully make her hair look not quite okay—to help free herself from what others think. Naturally she had a lot of resistance, but after she tried it a few times, she found it so freeing she started doing an occasional "bad-clothes day" as well. Not *needing* to look a particular way gives us a direct taste of the freedom of no one special to be.

I remember when one of my daughters, who was around five at the time, became very enthusiastic about dressing herself. She would put on four or five outfits at a time, each one layered on top of the other so you would see just parts of each blouse or dress. The problem, from my small-minded point of view, was that she looked so strange, and at first I was a little embarrassed. But she was so excited about her outfits that I started to look anew, and I saw that she had her own aesthetic, which was actually quite pleasing. The point is, on a very simple level, she was living authentically—not according to the convention of how she was supposed to look but according to her own inner sense. What's so sad is that we lose this naturally open mind as we grow older and we become more and more concerned with fitting in, with looking "right." Our self-image becomes our master.

One of my favorite aphorisms goes, "Dropping our facades, our identities, our stories—what remains? The answer: just being."

Where this gets difficult is when it gets close to home. An example is from John Lennon's song "Imagine": "Imagine there's no countries . . . / Nothing to kill or die for / And no religion too." He was describing the freedom of giving up our fixed views, even on the things we take most for granted, such as our so-called patriotism or our religious views. Or our most cherished facades and self-images. Or the stories we cling to as "our truth"—such as the story "I need someone to take care of me," or "Life is too hard," or "I'm worthless." An excellent question to ask ourselves is, "Who would I be without this story? This belief? This identity? This fear?" This question takes courage, because we have to look beyond the safety of the familiar. But living just for safety is dangerous—dangerous to living authentically!

It also takes honesty and precision to look at ourselves deeply, because we are identified with these views, stories, and self-images as the unassailable truth. These things serve as a subtle barrier to experiencing our natural being, our most authentic self. This is why so much emphasis has to be placed on objective self-observation. Especially when we're in the midst of discomfort, we need to ask, "What is my most believed thought right now?" Once we see the thought clearly, our identification with our emotional state begins to lessen. To help diminish this identification with the narrow subjective experience of being a "Me" even further, we can label our experience and thereby make it more objective. For example, if we find that we're hurt or afraid, instead of thinking, "I'm hurt" or "I'm afraid," we can say, "There is hurt" or "There is fear." In so doing we are no longer equating "I" with hurt or fear. We can even use this technique with physical discomfort. Instead of saying, "I have a headache" or "My back hurts," we can say, "There is pain." In using this simple approach we can begin to free ourselves from our intense identification with our emotions and even with our body. Sometimes just repeating the phrase "No one special to be" can break our identification with whatever emotion or story we're caught in.

Once we have objectified our thought process, in order to free ourselves even more completely, we must bring awareness to what it feels like, physically, to be caught in "Me." We ask ourselves, "What is this?" or "What is this experience?" We then focus like a laser on the subjective experience of living in the narrow inner sphere of "Me-ness." What does it actually feel like, very specifically, to be holding on to an opinion, or to be caught in a self-image or an emotion?

When we do this repeatedly, the sense of who we are, with all of our stories, loses its substantiality, its heaviness. There is a transformation out of the narrow subjective sphere into a more open experience of reality. When we bring awareness to our cherished self-images, such as our need to be special, they begin to lose their power over us. No longer puffing ourselves up or trying to stand out means we're coming closer to living like a white bird in the snow. That is, we no longer feel the inner compulsion to see ourselves or be seen in a particular way—there is no ulterior agenda. The result is true humility—no one special to be.

To be no one special means we are psychologically free of the illusion of "I-as-a-Me"—no longer seeing ourselves as a unique self, independent of the world around us. Not holding on to any particular view or opinion, or the stories about our past and who we are, or the many self-images and identities we use to define our "Me"—what remains? The presence of just being. This gives us an experiential taste of our most authentic self, with the inner knowing that who we truly are—our basic connectedness—is more than just our self-images, our stories, our body.

We can then begin to relate to the clouds of "Myself" as just clouds. We don't have to try to stop the clouds any more than we have to try to stop our thoughts. They don't go away, but there's a vast difference between identifying with the clouds and identifying with the vast sky within which the clouds appear. Identifying with the presence of just being, rather than identifying with "I-as-a-Me," is like identifying with the sky, and from that awareness the clouds are never as real or as substantial as they appear from the inside. As awareness opens up, the objective fact of our basic connectedness becomes more than just an intellectual understanding.

8

Who's Who in the Zoo?

A student comes in for an interview with his Zen teacher and tells the teacher how angry he is at his boss. The teacher interrupts him and asks, "Who's angry?" The student replies, "What do you mean?" And again the teacher asks, "Who's angry?" The frustrated student says, "I don't know." At which point the teacher rings his bell, signaling an end to the interview.

A week later the student returns, and the teacher sees that the student appears to be very relaxed. The teacher asks the student how the situation with his boss is going. The student smiles and says, "Oh, I'm not angry anymore." The teacher immediately asks, "Who's not angry?" The student doesn't respond, so the teacher again asks, "Who's not angry?" The student replies, "I don't know what you're asking." Whereupon the teacher again rings his bell.

The next week the student returns, and the teacher can see that the student appears to be visibly anxious. But the teacher is also impressed that the student had the courage to return, so he smiles at the student and says, "Today we're going to talk about who's who in your little zoo."

Who we think we are—that is, how we see ourselves—determines how we live our lives. If we don't know who we are, we will no doubt live our lives blindly. Conversely, knowing how to live most genuinely comes from uncovering the "who." In other words, we have to clarify with precision our many "Me's"—who's who in our little zoo. Once we uncover our various identities and behavior patterns, we can begin to work with the fears that drive them; and as we free ourselves from our fears, we come closer to living from our most authentic self. This type of honest looking at ourselves and our patterns is not easy, and often we prefer to remain complacent or in the dark.

Most of us, most of the time, are content to blindly skate on the thin ice, taking our life for granted. We choose patterns or strategies of behavior to try to control our world—in part, to help us avoid the anxious quiver in our being. We all have strategies that we're familiar with, such as trying harder or seeking diversions. We use these to skate along, hoping to avoid having to feel the fears that we don't want to address—such as the fears of loss of control, of failure, of being unworthy, of being alone, and so on. Rarely do we question our strategies; usually we just follow them blindly. But in following them we limit ourselves and define our own boundaries, and our life narrows down into a sense of vague dissatisfaction.

We have to start from the premise that we don't really know ourselves very well. Knowing ourselves involves clarifying all the ways we're run by the self-centered mind. This means we have to uncover our most basic identities and beliefs, observe our typical strategies of behavior, and perhaps most important of all, become very familiar with our fears. The clarification of what makes a "Me" is not a philosophical or theoretical inquiry;

the work has to be very specific, very empirical. For example, we have to clarify our thinking by knowing, with precision, what our actual beliefs are. This does not necessarily involve looking at our past, or analyzing why we think the way we do. The process of coming to know ourselves more deeply is an objective process, where we simply notice the present content of the mind, so that we can learn to see our thoughts *as* thoughts, and not as The Truth. The same holds as we observe our strategies: instead of analyzing why we behave the way we do, we simply look at our patterns of behavior and learn to see them as the conditioned behaviors that they are. This allows us to break our intense identification with our various "Me's."

One aspect of seeing who's who in our zoo is to look at our own complex of behavior patterns and see if we can discern a unifying thread. A good way to uncover this thread is to ask ourselves, "What is the most significant thing about me?" This is not an easy question to answer, since we are usually blind to our own primary feature. Further, this most significant or unifying thread always has both a positive and a negative side. For example, one person might describe their primary feature as "I try hard." This statement certainly captures the positive side, which is the natural desire to be productive, but at the same time it masks the fear of failure that may underlie it.

When we ask ourselves, "What is the most significant thing about me?" we may see more than one major basic behavioral strategy. This is not unusual; however, there are rarely more than two predominant patterns. The tricky part is to look for your own primary feature without getting caught in analysis or excessive thinking about yourself. The actual practice is to ask the question at various points throughout the day: "Who do I think I am right now?" If the answer is not readily apparent, we don't dwell on it; we simply return to objectively observing ourselves again and again until the answer becomes clear. Until we uncover our most deeply seated beliefs and patterns, they will continue to unconsciously dictate how we live.

The descriptions that follow are of our major belief-based strategies. As you read about them, see if you can recognize which ones best describe your primary feature. The descriptions will also include the fear or motivation that may, in part, underlie each strategy. These descriptions will be brief and are not an in-depth exploration. Still, they can serve as a basic guideline for looking inward.

Trying to make the world a better place, trying to make things right. The most significant self-concept is, "I live from conscience." The positive side is obviously the belief that things can be made better. The negative side is that this impulse can become very self-righteous and moralistic. The underlying motivation may be the wish to avoid the fear that things will never be right, particularly that "I" will never be right. This is the basic strategy of perfectionism.

Giving or nurturing, with the primary self-concept best described as "I'm a helper." The positive side comes from the natural generosity to give of oneself; the negative side is giving in the hope of being needed and appreciated. The motivation is to avoid the fear of being unloved. This is the basic strategy of the helper.

Achievement, getting ahead. "I try hard" is the most significant feature, and the positive side is that this behavior can bring success and productivity. The negative side is the need to be well regarded—geared to overriding the nagging sense of inadequacy, unworthiness, and failure. This is the strategy of trying to be on top of things, or at least appearing to be on top.

Trying to understand our feelings and to search for what is missing. The most significant belief about oneself is "I'm unique." On the positive side there is the ability to feel things deeply, and perhaps to express oneself creatively and artistically. The negative side is the tendency to dramatize suffering and to elevate oneself in one's uniqueness. The motivation is a craving for acknowledgment, to cover over the sense of being hopelessly flawed. This is the basic strategy of the romantic—trying to feel special.

Observing and understanding the world, with the goal of maintaining order and self-sufficiency. The primary self-concept is, "I'm the one who knows." The positive side is the ability to see reality objectively and clearly. The negative side is the tendency to hold oneself back and shut life out or withdraw, partly to ward off the fear of danger and chaos. This is the strategy of the observer.

Conformity and compliance—seeking the comfort of fitting in or following authority. The chief feature or self-concept is "I'm reliable," and it often involves the positive traits of being dutiful and responsible. This strategy is motivated by the need to avoid the fears of insecurity and groundlessness; and sometimes the strategy flips from the "fitting in" of conformity to the negative traits of doubting and yes-butting. However, the basic motivation of each is the need for security.

Keeping busy, and seeking adventure, diversion, or pleasure. The most significant belief about oneself is "I keep things lively, interesting, and enjoyable." The positive side is an optimistic and energetic ability to contribute; the negative side an endless seeking after busyness and entertainments, to avoid discomfort and to fill in the holes of longing and loneliness. This is the basic strategy of the adventurer.

Appearing strong and self-reliant, with the primary self-concept being "I'm in charge." The positive side is an ability to be direct, decisive, and protective of others. The negative side is a tendency to be domineering and combative. The basic motivation is to avoid the inner terror of feeling or appearing weak. This is the strategy of the asserter.

Being laid back and detached, with the most significant self-concept being "I keep the peace." The positive side is the ability to keep things mellow, while the negative side is a tendency to avoid engagement and commitment, often out of the fear of confrontation and rejection. This is the strategy of the peacemaker.

Hopefully you can see your own patterns in these admittedly brief descriptions. Once we recognize our own strategies, we need to ask ourselves, "Are any of these strategies really successful?" In general, the answer is yes, in that they can help us negotiate our way through our complex world; as well, they can temporarily keep our fears at bay. Yet when they fail, we can see how close we really are to the ever-present danger of falling through the thin ice.

The important thing is seeing whether we understand how to work with these strategies. The first thing that's required is that we be able to recognize our disappointments for what they are—the emotional reactions that we feel when our strategies don't really work in getting us the comfort that we want. And then, very specifically, we need to be able to see our disappointments as our path—in other words, we use our discomforts as our wake-up. Wake up to what? First, waking up to what's actually happening—seeing where we're blindly caught in our conditioned patterns. For example, we can ask ourselves where are we just trying to look good, or to seek approval, or to fulfill our attachments or cravings—for food or pleasure or comfort in any form? Where are we trying to avoid feeling anxiety or insecurity through trying to control and manipulate our world? This may require acknowledging the sense of entitlement that underlies our strategies—for example, the entitlement that we *should* we appreciated, that we shouldn't have to be uncomfortable, or that life shouldn't be so difficult. Wherever we are stuck in belief-based patterns, the practice is always to see that stuck place as our path. For example, if our strategy is that of the helper, what happens when we don't get appreciated for offering our help? We usually become angry or feel hurt. But if we remember to see our reaction as our path, it's as if a mirror is being held up to us, saying, "Here, look at your anger: it is showing you exactly where you are stuck in believing you need appreciation to prove your worth."

Once we recognize our disappointment over the fact that our patterns are not working the way we'd like, the practice is to refrain from replaying the strategies. Even though the strategies don't really work, our human tendency is to keep doing them over and over, like a rat in a maze. So refraining from the replay is a big step.

The next step, perhaps even more difficult than refraining, is to open to feeling the fear that drives the strategy in the first place. This definitely takes patience and perseverance, because another of our human tendencies is to turn away from our fears. Yet practice asks us to turn toward them—which simply means being open to actually feeling them, and to residing in the discomfort as best we are able in order to become free.

Please remember: When we feel discomfort or anxiety, we almost always think that something is wrong. The immediate tendency is to pursue our conditioned strategies—trying harder, hiding, or seeking escape—hoping that we can get away from the discomfort or anxiety. But the mere fact that we feel anxious doesn't necessarily mean that something is wrong. The only thing it means is that we're feeling anxious. In other words, we're simply having a conditioned response.

So instead of following our usual strategies, the practice is to first *recognize* what's going on—that is, to see our anxiety as just a conditioned response. And second, to *consciously refrain* from immediately engaging in our strategies of control and escape. This allows us to take the third and transformative step of *returning* to and residing in our experience itself, where we can begin to get a taste of the real freedom that arises from the power of awareness itself. My wife and fellow teacher, Elizabeth Hamilton, refined this practice and gave it the acronym "RRR," as a reminder of these three steps—Recognize, Refrain, and Return. Through this threefold process the ground is laid for being able to live more genuinely.

It is so very easy to lose sight of our spiritual path and just fall back into complacency and ease—the kind of false complacency that is sustained through our habitual strategies of behavior. We have to understand that even though our complacency keeps us asleep, and even though our discomforts can be our teacher, we have much less aversion to our complacency than we do to our discomforts. To live most authentically, we need to learn to fear our complacency far more than we fear our discomfort and distress.

9

The Misguided Quest

When I was partway through writing my first book, which was eventually published as *Being Zen,* I sent the first few chapters to a large publisher, certain that they would agree to publish the book. When I got the rejection letter back, along with the note saying they didn't think there was a market for my subject, I was both shocked and disappointed. My self-judgmental mind took the rejection as proof that I was somehow fundamentally lacking, and the disappointment quickly spiraled down into a feeling of doom. To avoid having to feel this, I immediately began the misguided quest to measure up—strategizing how to revise the book to make it fit the prevailing market.

Fortunately, after a day of this I realized what I was doing: I was considering forsaking what I truly wanted to write just to measure up and achieve external success—all to avoid having to feel the pain of unworthiness. Instead, I began to meticulously observe my mind. Interestingly, the two strongest believed thoughts were the self-judgment "I'll never measure up" and the counterstrategy "I *must* measure up." As it became clear that these two beliefs were two sides of the same basic fear of not being enough, the practice also became clear: to willingly reside in the physical experience of fear itself. As the fear became less and less solid, I no longer felt driven by the need to measure up in order to avoid feeling the fear, nor did the negative self-judgment seem so true. As I resumed my writing, I felt much freer of the attachment to outcome and more willing to write what I genuinely had to say, regardless of success.

Almost everyone lives out of this misguided quest to measure up. We may not expect life to be perfect, but we often expect others, and especially ourselves, to measure up. This quest is often not on the conscious level; in fact, many of us might deny that we even have it. But on an unconscious level—the level that dictates how we feel and act—the need to prove our worth is much more obvious.

Every time we are disappointed in ourselves, it's like a mirror being held up to us, showing us how we've been living out of the belief or expectation that we need to be better, that we shouldn't make mistakes or be flawed—in short, that we should measure up to some undefined ideal. This may sound like an unreasonable thing to believe in, and on some level it is; however, we need to remember that this belief is often not a conscious one.

How did this belief, this quest, arise? Let's speculate a little. There's no doubt we came out of the womb with the unspoken pain of separation, as well as the pains of being born. To interpret and make sense of this pain, very early on we construct the judgment, the belief, that we're basically flawed in some way. But this is not something we can easily live with, so to counter the belief that we're basically lacking, the ego gives us a way to control it and overcome it: it tells us we must measure up. As we make efforts to avoid feeling the original pain of separation, every time we falter, the small mind of the ego is there with a self-judgment: "You must do better!" This whole dynamic is based on the belief that we are fundamentally lacking in some way, coupled with the consequent quest to avoid feeling the discomfort this brings up.

Is this an accurate interpretation of how things actually evolved? Truthfully, I don't know for certain. But does it really matter? Does it matter anymore than it matters whether our personal "stories" are true—about why I'm the way I am or who's to blame. The only thing we can experience and work with is what our life is right now; and one thing that is certain is that, regardless of the exact cause, we judge ourselves mercilessly for not being enough.

This belief that we're fundamentally lacking is not new; it probably goes all the way back to the belief in original sin. Over time we've given it a little more psychological sophistication by giving "sin" some new names: being unworthy, flawed, neurotic, not enough, and so on. Nor is the concept that we have to measure up a new one. Every religion and every morality has some version of "You must do better!" This explains why guilt and especially shame are so much a part of religion and morality. Shame tells us that we're basically defective, and that the only way out of this uncomfortable condition is to pursue the quest of measuring up.

The deep-seated belief that we're not enough doesn't seem to substantially diminish regardless of how much success we have or how well we are regarded. Perhaps this belief has become so deeply a part of our conditioning that it's an integral part of what it feels like to be a "Me." Even when we're not in touch with the sense of our imagined inadequacy, it's still there, lurking. We can prove ourselves, improve ourselves, tell ourselves that everything is okay; nonetheless, the judgment that we'll never quite measure up still remains, almost as if it's embedded in our cells.

Let's look at this from a slightly different point of view. When a difficulty arises, we almost always think something is wrong. Often fears will be triggered; for example, we fear that we'll get hurt, or that things will fall apart. These fears often take us back to our fundamental pain of separation. It's a given that humans don't want to feel this discomfort, so to counter having to feel these fears, we try to find a way to address the situation. We instinctively seek ways to find safety and comfort, to take away whatever we see as "wrong," So we ask ourselves, "How can I fix it?" "How can I measure up?" This whole dynamic begins with the belief that something is wrong; and often, when we judge or believe that something is wrong, we conclude that something is wrong with *us*. In other words, at the root of our fixing pattern is the self-judgment of our own unworthiness. Our negative self-judgments have many flavors—feeling unworthy, stupid, incompetent, unappealing, or, more generically, that we're simply not enough.

As we already saw, our deep-seated self-judgments arise early on from the inevitable pain of our formative years. Over time, these judgments become more and more deeply ingrained, until eventually we regard them as the unquestioned Truth. Until we begin the work of honestly observing ourselves, these negative, painfully demeaning self-judgments may not even be open to question.

For example, the deeply embedded judgment "I'm unworthy" may not be on the surface of our thoughts, and may even be covered over by self-confidence. Yet because we don't want to feel the pain of this belief, it may nevertheless impact the way we relate to the world. Often our self-judgments act like radar; in other words, we perceive things based on what we believe and expect to see. For instance, if we believe we're unworthy, all we have to do is have one small setback and we'll immediately conclude, "See, I'm not enough. I'll never measure up." Consequently, these self-judgments guarantee that we'll stay stuck in our psychological pain. In every case, we're caught in the narrow, inaccurate confines of the thinking mind, and we believe in these judgments as the absolute truth. This perpetuates our suffering, and the cycle is vicious and relentless.

For some, a fundamental belief in their own unworthiness may drive them to be productive or to succeed, in order to compensate for this sense of inner lack. Others may withdraw or cease trying, in order to avoid risking failure. For many it surfaces through finding distractions or ways of numbing ourselves. In all of these cases, the motivation is the same: we don't want to feel the pain of believing we're not enough.

Our self-judgments are often below the level of awareness, but sometimes our negative self-judgments are also on the conscious, surface level. For instance, if we do something a little silly, the small mind of judgment is right on board to let us know about it. One of my students told me he realized his whole life had been about trying to get someplace, trying to be somebody. He said it seemed like it had been this way since he was a child. He realized his quest to measure up was mostly about trying to cover over a sense of lack—constantly judging himself for not being enough. A depiction of the extensiveness of our self-judgment was humorously portrayed in a *Peanuts* cartoon, where Charlie Brown was sitting on his bed thinking, "Sometimes I wake up at night and I ask, 'Where have I gone wrong?' Then a voice says to me, 'This is going to take more than one night.'"

Interestingly, our self-judgment can wreak havoc even during meditation. How many times have you judged yourself as a failure at meditation, simply because you had difficulty paying

83

attention? When I first started meditating, my self-judgmental mind had a field day. I had the expectation that if I were a good meditator, my mind would automatically become calm. An expectation like this, however, is a setup for both ongoing disappointment and unending self-criticism.

Self-judgment adds a whole extra layer of suffering on top of whatever pain we might already be feeling. Remembering Buddha's analogy of first and second arrows—he said if we're hit by an arrow, it will surely hurt, but if we're hit by a second arrow in the same spot, it will hurt much more. This may sound like common sense, but if we use the second arrow as an analogy to help clarify the harmful qualities of the judging mind, its meaning deepens and becomes more useful. For example, if we get a headache, there's no doubt it can be somewhat painful. But if we have the thought "This is terrible" or "Poor me," it's like being hit by a second arrow, and it may intensify the physical pain as well as adding emotional pain.

As we observe ourselves, we'll see that we shoot ourselves with second arrows quite regularly, even though we're normally not aware that we're doing this. Why? Because we identify with our thoughts and judgments as the unquestioned Truth. How many times, after making a mistake, which we can call the first arrow, do we add on the second arrow of self-judgment, "I can't do anything right"?

As we add on layers of self-judgment, we can easily become caught up in the desire to get away from all the yuckiness. At this point we automatically move into the fix-it mode, toward the misguided quest to measure up. Even after years of practice we may still be subtly caught in this quest. Even though life is continually telling us otherwise, we still believe, on some level, that we can finally measure up. Sometimes it's only when our body begins to age, despite our frantic efforts to exercise and diet our way back to youth, that we learn the unwanted lesson: that our desire to measure up and be in control will never be realized. Then we can finally understand that our belief that we have endless time to make things right is just an illusion, a fantasy.

This is where practice comes in. To work with the roots of self-judgment, we have to first refrain from the movement toward fixing our experience. This is not so easy, because the habit of fixing ourselves is so deeply ingrained in our conditioning. We get good at what we practice, and what we've been practicing our whole lives is trying to fix ourselves, trying to measure up. But once we've experienced the disappointment inherent in living this way, we may be motivated to actually refrain from the fixing pattern, at least on occasion.

Then, once we refrain, what's next? We become aware of how pervasive our self-judgments actually are. This is challenging, because these self-judgments are often one of the most elusive aspects of the thinking mind, and one of the last things we want to deal with. This is why relentless self-observation is so necessary. As with our other believed thoughts, we must first observe them with objectivity, labeling them for added clarity: "Having a believed thought *I'll never measure up*" or "Having a believed thought *I'm basically flawed.*" We may have to name our believed thoughts in this way many times before our investment in them, our identification with them, begins to diminish. The more we can see this pernicious pattern with some objectivity, the less we will identify with it as the reality of who we are.

This process of seeing ourselves more objectively also brings in the quality of kindness—which is the exact opposite of self-judgment—in that the increased objectivity allows us to see and relate to ourselves with more benign tolerance. We can then begin to cultivate a sense of space around our self-judgments, which allows us to stop struggling *against* ourselves. Perhaps we can learn to look at ourselves the way we look at a small child who is having difficulties. When we see a child struggling, we can readily understand that the child might be hungry, over-tired, or just a little cranky. We don't judge them as being defective, nor do we berate them for not measuring up.

When we can look at ourselves in the same way, we learn what it means to see our "stuff" as simply our conditioning, as *just* old wounds and deep beliefs. That allows us to be with *whatever* arises. It doesn't mean we like it, but we can relate to it in a new way. To soften around difficult self-beliefs is the path to truly understanding that these are not the deepest truths about us. As we learn how to make this soft effort around our relentlessly judging mind, we can relate in a new, more spacious way to the ancient wound of our seeming separateness. To be able to relate to the judging mind with the warmth of kindness is perhaps the single most potent antidote to our deep-rooted tendency to judge ourselves.

The next step is to directly feel the physical contraction in the thought-body connected with this belief. What does it feel like, physically, when we believe this thought? Is there a specific feeling in the body that accompanies our negative self-judgments? If we observe closely, the answer will be yes. The sensations, of course, are the feelings of fear and emotional pain that arise from deep within our conditioning—the pain of feeling basically alone and separate. This feeling of incompleteness is very unpleasant, and we will instinctively want to turn away from it, because we tend to want to avoid discomfort in any form. That's why the quality of perseverance is of key importance; we have to learn to just *stay*, even when our experience is not pleasing us in the ordinary sense. Put simply, the solution is never about fixing but rather about staying.

When we consciously reside in the physical feeling accompanying the belief in our fundamental separation, we gradually begin to recognize its insubstantiality. Staying fully present with this discomfort will often diminish it to the extent that it's no longer problematic. However, the objective is not to wage war with our judgments or with our discomfort, but to just observe and feel, as objectively as possible, what is happening *right now*. This is bound to require repeated efforts, since the patterns are so deeply embedded. What we're doing is learning to receive and include the whole of our being, just as it is, no longer judging, editing, rejecting.

I spoke earlier of my initial experiences in meditation, where I would be regularly disappointed by my spinning mind, judging myself and then trying harder, mostly unsuccessfully, to become calm. Now, many years later, there are still times when I sit down to meditate and my mind is all over the map. However, the difference now is that I am not particularly disappointed in myself. I don't judge myself as lacking, nor do I try to calm down. Instead, I just stay with the present-moment experience of scattered energy and thoughts. To really stay with scattered energy, without judgment, can actually bring a sense of equanimity.

Bringing conscious awareness to our self-judgment that we are fundamentally not okay allows us to see it for what it is—a deeply conditioned belief that causes not only suffering but also our endless and misguided quest to measure up. Yet as we feel into the roots of our suffering, not only does compassion for ourselves arise but also compassion for others who are caught in similar patterns of suffering.

As our understanding and compassion deepens, even though the self-judgments may still arise, we will no longer believe them as The Truth. You certainly don't have to accept this on faith. If you sincerely want to live more authentically, you can verify for yourself what is possible. Remember, it's a given that the mind will ceaselessly generate judgments. Yet with each un-examined judgment, and the consequent effort to measure up, we end up living a life that is neither real nor satisfying. This is the inauthentic subjective world of living from "Me." But ob-serving our patterns of judging and striving, and feeling how they impact the body, it becomes possible to open to the experi-ence of just being. Just as the judging mind and the need to measure up are at the root of our dissatisfaction, this underlying awareness of just being is one of the sources of our fundamental contentment. But to cultivate this awareness and to live a truly authentic life, we have to start by uncovering and working with the judgments and behaviors that block it.

10

Shades of Gray

There is a common tendency among human beings to see things in terms of black or white—in an attempt to simplify life and create the illusion that we understand things and are in control. But things are rarely simple—life comes to us much more in the form of complexity and continuums; and further, life is always changing. So it's important to look beyond our tendency to see things as black or white, and instead be aware that life appears in many shades of gray. This is particularly true when trying to learn to live more authentically, when we can easily get lost in confusion, especially in those areas where we don't see the subtle shades of gray in our own feelings and behavior.

EXPECTATION AND ASPIRATION

One of the main places we get confused is in not differentiating between expectation and aspiration. Everyone has expectations when they start practice, often in the form of hopes of becoming calm and peaceful. My expectation, and what drove me for many years, was that practice would help me become free from my fears. On the other hand, when we think about aspiration, we usually think about something higher than a personal expectation—a higher calling.

Yet the question might arise, Isn't our aspiration to wake up just another way of trying to fulfill our expectations that practice will take away our difficulties, and consequently make us feel better? This is an important question, and the best way to answer it is to look inside ourselves at our own experience. Sometimes it's difficult to tell what exactly is driving us; is it the small mind that just wants to feel better, or is it something deeper inside us?

One clue: being driven by expectations will almost always lead to disappointment. Why? Because it is not based on what life is, but on what we want life to be. For example, expectation, which is based in the mind, is often rooted in the ego-driven ambition to get something, such as enlightenment, or, at very least, to feel differently, namely calm, free from fear, or to appear wise. Sometimes practice may, in part, meet our expectations and thereby reinforce them. But when practice doesn't meet our expectations—that is, when we don't get what we want—we experience disappointment.

Having the expectation that we can be free from all of our problems can even lead to discouragement and depression, because it ignores the fact that life will never stop testing us with difficulties. Yet our disappointment, whether in the form of sadness, anger, self-pity, bitterness or whatever, is like a red flag. It is telling us to look more closely at what we're up to. What we'll see is that our expectations were an exact setup for our disappointment. This is why it's important to recognize where we're

caught in our expectations, or in feeling entitled to have life be
any particular way.

While expectation is based in the mind, we can say that aspiration is based in the heart, or in our essential nature. Aspiration has been described as our true nature striving to reveal itself. In other words, it can be seen as an inherent movement toward who we truly are, like an acorn becoming an oak tree. Conversely, the efforts of expectation are often characterized by ambition, neediness, and fear. The effort of aspiration is softer, not as driven by results as by the inner impulse to live more genuinely.

I remember sitting in Trinity Church on a trip to New York City fairly recently. I love to meditate in churches—there's something about the setting that I believe is very conducive to getting in touch with oneself. As I was sitting there, I wasn't thinking about anything in particular, and then out of the blue it hit me that what I most deeply wanted, what I have always wanted, ever since I began the path of meditation over forty years ago, is to simply dwell in the heart of awareness, and to live from that place. This includes living with kindness and gratitude, and being free of the constriction of attachment and fear. To me, this is what it means to live from aspiration, to live most authentically. It's not about getting somewhere or becoming someone else—it's about becoming who I most truly am.

Unfortunately, when expectations become dominant, our aspiration tends to get dwarfed. The small mind of the ego wants what it wants—often based in the desire for comfort and security—and it speaks with a louder voice than the softer voice of aspiration. But over time, particularly as we learn to be more inwardly quiet and open, we can hear the more deeply compelling message of our aspiration.

Often aspiration and expectation intertwine, and it may be

hard to know who's who in our internal zoo. This is why it's rarely black or white—one or the other. Yet an important part of the practice life is to continually feed the part of us that wants to wake up. Whether it's through meditation, prayer, reading, being in nature—we have to use whatever we can to nourish the aspiration that urges us to realize our true nature.

PERSONAL LOVE AND THE BIG LOVE

This one is very difficult to talk about, in part because there are many different forms of personal love. There is the love of a parent for a child, the love between friends, romantic love, sexual love, and others. Personal love always involves intense good feelings, and often a sense of connectedness. In some cases, particularly in romantic love, there is an accompanying flow of chemicals, such as dopamine and endorphins, that contribute to a very rosy view. Then, as the initial glow subsides, so does the flow of chemicals, and we can go from "roses, roses" to "thorns, thorns."

Personal love is always based on attachment to our feelings. In other words, it's predicated on the emotion-based belief that without this particular person I can't be happy. This form of clinging includes the enjoyment we get when we're with the person, as well as the angst we feel when we think of losing the person. But is attachment really love? Is it love when what we love is the idea of the person and what we believe they can give us, and not the actual person? Is it love when what we love is the feeling of love and not the actual person? Is it love when we believe we can't live or be happy without the person? Isn't this much closer to neediness and fear than it is to love?

It's important to acknowledge up front that most of us are going to have—or want—personal love. This is normal. We just need to see it for what it is. Now let's compare personal love to Big Love, the love that is our true nature. This Big Love is very hard to talk about without getting theoretical. But if you've experienced this, it becomes clear that there are certain qualities that are quite different from our normal experience of personal love. One quality of Big Love is that it is all-embracing—that is, it includes everyone and everything. Like the sun's rays shining on everyone equally, regardless of good or bad, the experience of Big Love is not directed toward just one person.

Nor does it ask for something in return. In personal love there is always the expectation that we'll get something—attention, security, emotional gratification, pleasure, and on and on. There is an unspoken bargain: if you don't give me what I want I won't give you what you want. But in Big Love there are no expectations of reward; the love is given freely—freely in the most literal sense.

Big Love is also not personal—that is, it is not exactly about "Me." There is not the thought that *I* am loving, or that my love deserves merit. The only way to put this is, "Big Love simply *is*." This is why we say that Big Love is the natural state of our being, when our personal needs, agendas, and fears no longer block it.

It's easy to lose sight of even the possibility of Big Love, even though it is the fruit of living most authentically, most in touch with our true nature. We are seduced again and again by the promise of personal love, in spite of all the disappointment and anguish and fear that is so much a part of the personal-love dynamic. Where the shades of gray appear is in the experience of connectedness that is common to both personal love and Big Love. But once we have enough tastes of Big Love, it gets easier to see the difference—the connectedness of personal love is very small and subjective, always directed toward another person, whereas the sense of connectedness in Big Love is more global and inclusive.

Recently, when I was out for a cup of coffee with Elizabeth, I ate a rather big piece of chocolate. Twenty minutes later, when the chemicals hit, I felt full of love and the feeling of connectedness. In other words, I was feeling personally very happy in the moment. But even though it felt close to Big Love, in truth, I knew it was just an ephemeral feeling. It certainly felt good and there was nothing wrong with it, but it was clear that the feeling was dependent on my having had a good day as well as a good dose of chocolate. It was also clear that the love I was experiencing wasn't the state of Being that is revealed when our fears and stories and agendas drop away—where we experience the freedom of just being, where the love includes everyone and everything.

Again, there's nothing wrong with personal love, other than that it is often based in ever-changing external conditions—sometimes something as simple as a piece of chocolate. We can still enjoy it and appreciate it, as long as we understand it for what it actually is, and as long as we can remain open to the bigger love that is our true nature. The question is, how long will we go on living a life where Big Love is not a real part? How long will we settle for just the pleasure of personal love? To live most authentically requires working with whatever blocks the love that is our true nature from coming forth.

LETTING GO AND LETTING BE

"Letting go" is one of the most popular phrases in spiritual practice. It is even common in everyday usage. Basically, letting go means that we can, and should, drop something that is not good for us, such as a harmful attitude or a burdensome emotion.

Often the advice to "let something go" is well intentioned, and certainly we can occasionally unburden ourselves by just letting go. But usually the things we can simply let go of are very small. For example, if the Yankees, which are my favorite baseball team, lose a game, it is fairly easy for me to shrug it off and not wallow in upset. However, when it comes to deep-seated emotions or deeply conditioned attitudes, the idea of letting go is, for me, more wishful thinking than it is a realistic possibility.

If we could simply just let go of things we don't like or find unhelpful, we would already be quite happy! Just think about the last time you were really angry at someone. Think about how you were much more interested in being right than you were in letting go of your anger. If someone said to you, "Just let go of your anger"—how easy would it be to do that? It gets even more difficult to let go when dealing with our most deeply conditioned patterns and fears. Trying to let go is, in a subtle way, the same as trying to get rid of the things we don't like, especially the thoughts and feelings we find difficult to feel. We're seeing them as the enemy and wanting life to be different.

Letting be may sound similar, but it is actually quite different. Letting be means we don't try to drop it (let it go), nor do we try to alter it or force ourselves to accept it. Rather we simply acknowledge what's there and say yes to it, which means that we're willing to feel it, just as it is. We don't have to like it, nor, on the other hand, do we have to view it as an obstacle or an enemy—we just have to be willing to experience exactly what our life is right now.

Instead of seeing it as the enemy, we see it as our path, which is a critical difference. Interestingly, when we can truly let something be, it will often let go on its own, without any effort on our part to make that happen. In fact, the effort to make it happen—the attempt to let go—will often guarantee the opposite.

It is certainly a good idea to have the intention to free ourselves from our fears and our conditioning. This intention, in part, is what, is behind the wish to let go of things. But having the intention and actually bringing it to fruition are two different things. To bridge the gap between the two, between wanting to live most authentically and being able to drop what prevents it, we need to learn what it means to truly let life be.

It's important to remember that the ego mind will consistently try to pervert our best practice intentions. It's predictable and inevitable that this will happen. The point is not to get caught in the ego's black-or-white thinking, where we tend to remain confused, or at least unclear. When we are more precise in our observations, we can watch and learn—and get an inward feel for the subtle shades of gray between black and white, between expectation and aspiration, personal love and Big Love, letting go and letting be. In this way we can better understand what we're doing on the path toward learning to live more genuinely.

PART THREE

Emotional Awakening

11

The Dilemma of Anger

Here's an interesting question: why do we continue to do things that are harmful to us? The perfect example is anger. One of my students, who is a psychologist, told me how frustrating it is to work with patients who are habitually angry. Even when they would acknowledge her good suggestions to work with the anger, they nonetheless wouldn't do what she suggested. It reminds me of a line from a poem by W. H. Auden: "We would rather be ruined than changed." The fact is, when we express our anger, it doesn't just go outward—it is also toxic to us; holding on to our anger is like eating bad food. We can all probably recognize this tendency in ourselves—to continue to hold on to our anger internally and express it outwardly—even though we know it undermines our aspiration to live more openly and genuinely.

In part, living from anger is sustained by the illusion that we have endless time. We continue to let anger get the best of us because we don't yet truly realize that our life is precious and limited. Instead, we blindly indulge our entitled belief that life owes us something. Even when we see how our angry emotional reactions separate us and keep us closed, we hold on to this restricting emotion with a puzzling tenacity.

What is anger really about? When life doesn't give us what we want, we usually react. For example, when we have an expectation or a strong desire, we will feel dissatisfaction if our expectation or desire is not fulfilled. We cling to the entitled belief that life should go the way we want it to go. And when life doesn't go that way, anger says, "No! I want what I want!" This is not only true in our big explosions of anger. We can be angry in the form of irritability if our computer starts malfunctioning. We can be angry in the form of impatience if we have to wait in line at a store. We can be angry in the form of frustration if our political party suffers a defeat. We can be angry in the form of indignation and self-righteousness if someone criticizes us.

Again the question, Given that we hurt ourselves and others with our anger, why is it so difficult to stop expressing it? In a way the answer is simple: we *want* to be angry, because the small mind of anger wants nothing more than to be right. There's a feeling of juiciness and power that accompanies the expression of anger, and this feeling can be quite intoxicating.

Seen from an evolutionary point of view, cultivating our anger makes even more sense. There was a time when our raw instinctual reactions served a real purpose: to help us ward off physical threats in order to survive. The fact that we no longer face the same kinds of danger that we did as cavemen doesn't seem to matter—our bodies and minds have not yet caught on. Even though the anger no longer serves us in the same way, the powerful, even "good" feeling of anger remains. This is the dilemma of anger: even though it undermines our aspiration to live a more authentic life, it is reinforced in the body as something desirable.

Anger is also reinforced in another, equally powerful way: it can shield us from feeling the hurt and fear that are often right below the surface of anger. For example, if someone criticizes us and we feel hurt, we may immediately move into self-righteousness and blaming in order to avoid having to experience the more vulnerable feeling of being hurt. Also, we may experience anger in the form of rage when we feel powerless, such as when our remote control stops working or when someone cuts us off on the highway. Rage gives us a false feeling of power and control, yet it is often a way of avoiding feeling the fear we don't want to feel.

There comes a critical point on the practice path when we finally realize to what extent anger adversely impacts our life. This is not the same as simply feeling guilty about being angry. Guilt is another, more subtle form of anger, turned inward at ourselves. Nor is it about the moral injunction "Don't be angry." The deeper realization of the need to turn away from anger usually comes from the genuine remorse that results from realizing that we're disconnected from our true nature. We no longer want to perpetuate the suffering that so often results from our anger. Nor do we want to live a life based just on our attachment to life going a particular way. It is a sure sign that our practice is maturing when we develop the willingness to be with our life as it is rather than how we want it to be.

It's at this point in practice that the question arises, how can I effectively work with my anger? Over the years of clarifying my own work with anger it has become clear that what is needed is a step-by-step approach. The experience I've gleaned, both from working with myself and from working with others for the past twenty years, has helped me refine this step-by-step approach in a way that makes it accessible to anyone who is serious about working with their anger. It is based on the five basic questions that were discussed in chapter 4, and it has proven to be very successful in helping people extricate themselves from their deeply entrenched patterns. However, this has also made it obvious that successfully working with anger can sometimes be a hit-or-miss proposition. We will occasionally fall back into our habitual patterns and perhaps even get swept up in an explosion of anger that seems to come out of nowhere. When this happens, it is easy to get discouraged; however, knowing that occasionally "failing" is part of the process can be helpful when we get stuck. It is also helpful to return again and again to remembering what we most truly want: to live authentically from our true nature.

Step 1: Recognizing

The first step in working with anger is recognizing that we are, in fact, angry. This is not as simple or as straightforward as it may sound. When I was in my thirties, my family used to call me the Black Cloud, based on my angry outbursts and moods. If I was asked, "Why are you angry?" I would angrily reply, "Who's angry?" We're often not aware that we're angry, particularly with the more subtle forms of anger such as impatience, irritability, and passive aggression.

Sometimes we may feel that something is off but still not see clearly what is going on. In order to recognize where we are caught, we can ask the practice question "What's actually going on right now?" We usually don't see the difference between the three components of our experience: first, the *objective situation;* second, our *emotional reaction* to that situation; and third, the *behaviors* that arise from our reaction. Usually these three components seem to blend into an indistinguishable whole without much clarity. For example, let's say we're waiting in a traffic jam and getting very hot under the collar. What is actually going on? *Objectively,* the main thing going on is that we're sitting in a car. We add the *emotional reaction* of impatience, and then out of that we may find ourselves indulging the *behavior* of slamming the steering wheel or cursing out loud. This example is a simple one, and here we probably know we're angry. Yet even here we may not distinguish between the objective situation, our reaction, and our behavior. In more subtle examples, our anger might not be that obvious. This is why it's helpful, whenever we feel caught or confused, to ask the simple question "What is actually going on right now?"

Asking this question can also help us clarify the subtleties in our own behavior. For example, if we were brought up being taught that it's not okay to be angry, the chances are strong that we'll suppress our feelings. This is true even if we're aware that suppressing feelings is not good for us, either physically or emotionally. A subtle variant of this can sometimes be seen even in established meditators. Such suppression gets justified because of an ideal image of ourselves as someone who is above anger. But whether we bypass our anger in this unskillful way or seek diversions, such as the Internet or overeating, we do not free ourselves from anger by pushing it out of awareness. It continues to imprint on us, festering inside as unhealed pain. Sooner or later it will arise—perhaps as passive aggression, depression, or even an explosion of rage.

The more common behavior that arises from anger is expression. We can express our anger in one of two ways: First, we can express it internally through thinking or ruminating. This is what it means to wallow in anger. Second, we can express it externally through blaming and self-justification. We all know the experience of the forceful determination to be right, to prevail. Interestingly, whether we suppress our anger or express it, internally or externally, we are rarely in touch with what is actually going on within us. This is why it's so important to start with the step of asking, "What is actually going on right now?"

STEP 2: REFRAMING

After recognizing our anger and seeing how it plays out in our behavior, the second step in working with anger is to see the anger as our path. In a way, we're not doing anything other than reframing how we relate to what we're experiencing. Instead of justifying our anger, or seeing it as an obstacle, we understand that the anger is pointing us in the direction of awakening. It is telling us to look inward, to see how anger captures us in a self-protective cocoon. It's also an invitation to look at our expectations and requirements out of which the anger is born. But to see our anger as our path requires a degree of courage—to be willing to feel what's there rather than get pulled back into self-justification and blaming. Reframing how we relate to our anger is like turning our old views right side up; what we once saw as a flaw we now see as an opportunity to go deeper into our life.

STEP 3: CLARIFYING

In order to abandon blaming and justifying, which are the powerful protective strategies that continue to fuel the anger, it is usually necessary to clarify what we're thinking and believing. Anger is often born out of our beliefs, particularly our expectations. In a way, our expectations are a setup for our angry reactions. For example, if we have the expectation that life should be fair, when we encounter something that seems to us to be unfair, our automatic reaction will be anger. Yet in the moment of anger we may not even be aware that we have this expectation. This is where thought labeling comes in. Thought labeling allows us to clarify the thoughts and expectations we have on board with a degree of precision. For example, "Having a believed thought this isn't fair." "Having a believed thought people are stupid." When we label thoughts in this way, we break our identification with the thoughts as The Truth, and unless we do this, it will be very difficult to practice effectively with anger.

Sometimes our thoughts may lie below the surface of awareness, and it may not be obvious what we're believing. Even after we ask, "What is the most believed thought right now?" we may not get a clear answer. Sometimes asking, "How is it supposed to be?" will point us to exactly where we are stuck in an expectation or entitlement. For example, if we have the belief that people should be trustworthy and do what they say they will do, we are bound to sooner or later experience the anger of disappointment. We may feel totally justified in our anger, but the fact is, regardless of what another person did or didn't do, it's still *our* anger. This doesn't mean there shouldn't be any consequences if people break their word, but it doesn't alter the fact that if we're angry, we need to address it within ourselves.

Situations like this are often very messy, and there is rarely clarity about what we're actually believing. This is why it can be so helpful to ask, "How is it supposed to be?" When we see our own part, we realize that our anger was a direct result of having a particular expectation—in this case, that people *should* be trustworthy. Remember, the emphasis is on becoming free from our own conditioning—our angry reactions—not what may need to be done in our interactions.

If we don't clarify the mind, then each time we replay a thought, particularly of blame, it's like throwing a log on a fire.

EMOTIONAL AWAKENING

Each thought fuels the fire of anger and makes it harder to get any clarity. This is why observing and clarifying the mind, including labeling our specific thoughts, is a critical step in working with anger.

STEP 4: EXPERIENCING

One of the most interesting aspects of the dilemma of anger is that when we're angry, we rarely actually experience what anger really is. We are either suppressing it or caught in expressing it, either in words and actions or in our thoughts of blame and resentment. Even when we express it and "feel angry," we are unlikely to actually feel the energy of anger physically. To be truly present, we need to reside in the essence of anger itself. This is why we ask the question "What is this?" or "What is this moment?" It allows us to focus like a laser on the energy and physical sensations of anger, minus the thoughts. The thoughts may still be running through the mind, but as we observe and label them, thereby putting space around them, we can then specifically feel what's there.

Experiencing anger in this way is actually a quiet process. Even when the anger is explosive, once we refrain from fueling the heat of anger with our thoughts, we can experience it as just energy and sensations. We focus in on the heat, the tightness, the pressure. What does it really feel like? Again and again we have to turn away from the blaming and resentful thoughts, and again and again we return to the physical experience in the body. It is here that we can begin to quietly explore the layers of emotion underneath our anger—the hurt, grief, and fear. Each layer requires the same experiential process—clarifying the mind and feeling the sensations and energy in the body.

106

Gradually, as we let ourselves experience what anger really is, it begins to transform, and we no longer identify with the emotion as "Me." We see that our most authentic self—our true self—is much bigger than the story of "Me" that we want to believe in.

It's important to remember and understand that experiencing anger in this way, by refraining from expressing it, is very different from suppression. Refraining is very specific: we're either refraining from thought patterns, such as our stories of blame and victimhood, or from our behavior patterns, such as lashing out or our addictive tendencies to escape. We refrain so we can actually feel what's there. When we suppress, we don't feel—we push the feelings down out of awareness. Suppression is often based in fear—the fear of being present with feelings we may want to avoid. Conversely, refraining is based in courage—the courage to feel what we may not want to feel, such as hurt, which may lie right below the anger. Suppression is the exact opposite of *experiencing*, and it is only by refraining from expressing our anger that we can actually experience it and put more space around it.

STEP 5: LETTING BE

The final step in working with anger is to let it be. When we get angry at life or at a person, where we want to lash out or blame, letting be may not seem like a realistic option. The powerful energy of anger may not seem amenable to quiet observation, and we're likely to resist sitting in meditation and just feeling what's there. This is why, in order to work effectively with anger, we first have to experience a degree of remorse for our own unkindness—the unkindness that arises when we express anger. It is also valuable to realize that when we get caught in anger, no matter how much we may feel that the anger is justified, the fact is that it is *we* who have lost sight of the path. It is we, when caught in the closed-heartedness of anger, who have lost our way.

Once we realize this, we are much more willing to decline the seductive call of blame and resentment—no longer using another's behavior to justify our anger. Instead we are willing to explore the experience of anger itself. This is how we learn to let the experience just be. As we let the experience just be, we can also explore our own unkindness toward the other, as manifested in our judging and blaming, our insistence on being right, and our elevating of ourselves and putting the other down. As we feel the remorse for our own unkindness more deeply, we may begin to see that the other did not intentionally mean to hurt us; it was just the unskillful act of someone in pain. From being present with our own pain, and letting it just be, we see that their pain and their struggle are no different from our own. This is how genuine compassion and forgiveness for ourselves and for others can arise naturally.

Letting be doesn't mean that we never take action. It does mean, however, that we don't act from the negativity of anger. Sometimes we might think that, in certain situations, we have to be angry in order to take action. For example, if we see an injustice, we believe that our anger is what pushes us to do something to remedy the situation. Yet from the point of view of practice, there is *never* a justification for anger, no matter how righteous we may feel.

Again, this doesn't mean that we shouldn't act; it means we can act without the negative aspect of our anger. When our behavior comes from the negative energy of anger, we are not acting from either clarity or compassion. We are more likely in the grip of fear, where we make others the enemy; and when caught in this narrow sense of "self," we have lost all sight of our basic connectedness. But as we enter deeply into practicing with anger, we can develop a sense of space around that narrow sense of "Me." As our anger begins to transform, the energy of anger is redirected into a sense of resolve, without the negative overlay of anger. It is from this resolve that we can engage in life with both action and a sense of clarity and compassion.

A One-Day Practice

One of the main difficulties in working with anger is that it often blindsides us, or arises suddenly right in the middle of messy and complex circumstances. At first, all we can do is to watch ourselves go through our familiar angry response. Hopefully we know enough to keep our mouth shut, to not cause further harm; or at least to apologize when the anger gets the best of us. However, it's possible to prepare for those situations where anger seems to go through us from out of nowhere.

I've been doing a practice for many years that I've found helps with this exact preparation. One day a week I devote the entire day to practicing what I call "Nonmanifestation of Anger." From the moment I wake up until the moment I go to sleep, I make a conscious effort not to express negative emotions, either externally or internally. Because I'm attuned to not expressing the anger, the moment it begins to arise, awareness is likely to kick in; and it's become easier to catch that point where I would normally choose to believe my thoughts, which fuels the expression of the anger. Interestingly, in refraining from the thoughts, sometimes the anger quickly dissolves, leaving little residue. In fact, it's actually quite amazing to see that our anger is almost always optional. In other words, this one-day practice helps us see what is possible: we can see that when anger arises, we have a *choice*, and that we can change our responses and behaviors.

Granted there are times when anger may arise very strongly, and it may not then readily dissolve, even if our choice is to refrain from indulging it. But if we make the effort not to let our thoughts get a toehold, and stay focused on feeling the physical energy of the emotion itself, the anger will often dissipate much more quickly than it normally would. This is especially true if we make use of the technique of breathing the energy of anger into the hara—a technique that is described in detail in chapter 5.

Even if the anger doesn't dissipate, there's another great benefit to this one-day practice of Nonmanifestation of Anger—we're much more likely to bring awareness to the root of our anger. Usually we're so caught up in the mushroom-cloud explosion of anger that there is little awareness of the fear out of which the anger often arises. For example, in the past, if someone used to cut me off on the freeway, I would usually react immediately with anger, sometimes even with rage. But since I've been doing this one-day practice, it's now much more likely that I'll catch a glimpse of the fear of danger that is right under the anger. It is only from repeated practice in refraining from expressing the anger that this deeper awareness becomes possible. Whatever else you get from this chapter, I strongly urge you to try this one-day practice of Nonmanifestation of Anger. If you do it one day a week for several months, regardless of the ups and downs that are inevitable with any new practice, it's very likely you will find that your relationship to your anger changes dramatically.

Along with this practice, we can continually keep in mind the five steps that help us work with our anger. First, *recognizing* it when it arises, including recognizing our typical patterns of reaction when we get angry, such as suppression, ruminating, lashing out. Second, *reframing* our anger so we don't see it as our enemy, but rather as our exact path to freedom. Third, *clarifying* the beliefs and expectations that are a setup for our anger. Fourth, bringing a focused awareness to the *physical experience* of anger itself—the sensations and energy. And fifth, *letting the whole experience just be,* which allows us to ultimately experience compassion for the pain that we all share.

Everyone struggles with anger—it's an integral part of the life of sleep, where we are often a slave to our mechanical reactions and behaviors. But it is possible to end the struggle and live a life that is relatively free from manifesting anger. It's not that anger won't ever arise, but rather that we'll be much less likely to get caught in it. What this requires, as much as anything, is the realization that we don't have endless time, at which point we can begin to truly commit to our life; that is, to living it as genuinely as possible. Living genuinely undercuts our narrow identification with "Me"—with my stories of entitlement, blame, and resentment. Resolving the dilemma of anger is one of the most satisfying fruits of a life of practice.

12

Saying Yes to Fear

Fear is what drives much of our behavior, and at the same time it is the one thing that we least want to feel. When I first started spiritual practice, I had the strong expectation that practice would free me from anxiety and fear. I thought that if I studied and meditated, and struggled to change my behaviors, I could replace the undesirable parts of myself with a new, improved version of me—namely, I'd be free of anxiety.

Early on I decided to confront my fears directly whenever they arose, thereby hoping to amputate them. For example, I'd wear clothes that didn't look good in order to confront my fear of disapproval. Or I'd force myself to speak publicly even though I had a strong fear of public humiliation. One time, my teacher suggested I sing a song on Fisherman's Wharf in San Francisco. I made up a Bob Dylan–like song, bought a black derby hat, and went to the area where there were crowds of tourists waiting for the cable cars to turn around. I remember being so petrified I thought I might even faint or throw up. But I was determined to smash through my fear, so I sang my song and then begged for money. After doing it several times it got increasingly easier, and I actually thought I had overcome my fear. But in truth, it was like cutting off a weed; the fear was temporarily removed, but because I had not gone to the root, it eventually returned.

This example illustrates two of the classic misconceptions about dealing with anxiety and fear. The first is seeing fear as the enemy, as a flaw within myself that I have to conquer. The second is believing that if I confront my fears and go against them, they'll go away permanently. There is also the more subtle version: if I have a deep spiritual practice, I can become free of fear altogether. It's understandable that we would hold on to these misconceptions, because we have so much aversion to feeling the discomfort of fear, and we'll do almost anything to avoid it and get rid of it. Yet it's also a fact that whenever we don't address our fear, we make it more solid, and consequently, our life becomes smaller, more limited, more contracted. In a way, every time we give in to fear, we cease to live genuinely.

What are we so afraid of? One of our most basic fears is the fear of loss of security, including the fear of disease and pain, as well as the fear of the loss of status and material security. We have a strong fear of powerlessness and loss of control, and for many, there is an equal fear of being controlled by others. There is the fear of abandonment and being alone, including the fear of the loss of loved ones. Another universal fear is that of unworthiness—of being found fundamentally flawed or not enough in some way. This is at the root of the fear of being criticized and the fear of looking foolish. And for some there is the fear of death, and maybe even more so, the fear of the suffering we expect will be involved in dying. For many people the strongest fear of all is the fear of fear itself.

Recent studies show that certain people are born with more sensitivity to external stimuli. You could say they have "thinner skins" and are thus more prone to being vigilant to signs of danger. What this means is that some people are physiologically more likely to experience anxiety and fear, and that others, who are born with less sensitivity to external stimuli, are physiologically less prone to experience as much fear. If we are the type with a fear-based temperament, it's important to understand that this is simply an inborn trait. When fear arises, it doesn't necessarily mean that something is wrong. Or that something is wrong with us. Or that we need to do anything about it.

Whether or not we are physiologically inclined to readily have fear come up, all of us have fears that are related to our psychological conditioning, that is, from events that happened to us early on. When our conditioning gets triggered, it will cause a fear response in the body. For example, if we feel we are criticized or judged, the body will react as if danger were present. This also occurs if we fear confrontation, or intimacy, or failure. When these situations arise, the body will sense danger and go into the fight, flight, or freeze mode—the adrenaline will start to flow, the heart will beat faster, and the muscles of the body will contract.

In order to avoid having to deal with these fears, we develop certain strategies very early on—strategies that become our basic way of relating to the world. For example, we learn to try harder, or to be pleasing, or to hide. My main strategy was to try harder; and even though it allowed me to achieve external success by driving me to excel, it never really worked, because it never addressed the core fear. This core fear, and all of the day-to-day anxiety that arose out of it, were only temporarily put at bay.

There's an alternative way to live—one that is no longer driven by fear. In fact, the essence of living authentically starts when we learn to relate to our fears in a new way: instead of seeing fear as our enemy, we can begin to see fear as a wake-up, a signal. This makes it an opportunity to see where we're stuck, where we're holding ourselves back, and where we can open more to life. We have to understand that fear is the protective cocoon of ego telling us to stop. It tells us not to go beyond the outer edge of our cocoon. But the direction of our path is to move directly *toward* our fears, for only in this way can we go beyond fear's cocoon. While we may not like it, fear can be our best indicator that we're going in the right direction. In fact, whatever we can't say yes to can be considered the exact direction of our path.

What does it actually mean to say yes to our fear? It means we're willing to open to it and embrace it as our path to freedom. Saying yes doesn't mean we like it—it simply means we're willing to feel what it really is. Saying yes to fear is the opposite of what we usually do, which is to run away from it. Yet when we stop resisting what is, and over time develop the genuine curiosity to know what's really going on, it's possible to begin to see our experience of fear almost as an adventure instead of as a nightmare. When fear arises, the mind of curiosity can say, "Here it is again—what will it feel like this time? It is also helpful to simply say, "There is fear," instead of the usual "I'm afraid." When we say, "I'm afraid," we solidify the narrow, subjective experience of fear, as well as the "Me" that identifies itself as a fearful person. But when we say, "There is fear," it puts some space around what might become a dark and claustrophobic feeling. This added space, along with the mind of curiosity, allows us to be less identified with the experience of fear, thus less caught in it.

To know what fear really is, whenever it arises, we ask the

question "What is this?" We're not asking why we have it or analyzing it—we're essentially asking, "What is this moment?" To answer, we simply have to look at two things: the fearful thoughts and the physical sensations of fear. The practice is to pause, allow ourselves to observe the thoughts racing through our mind, and feel the physical sensations and energy throughout our body.

Here's an example of the process: Several years ago I had to have a test done to determine if I had prostate cancer, and even though I didn't have any physical symptoms, the days of waiting for the results were fraught with anxiety. When I tried to observe the mind, at first it was hard to catch specific thoughts—it was more a vague sense of doom and danger. But then specific thoughts began to emerge: "I can't handle this." "What if I have cancer?" "What's going to happen to me?" These thoughts seemed so solid, so compelling; but by observing and labeling them again and again, their power began to dissipate.

Then I brought awareness to the physical experience in the body. This was particularly difficult, because the sensations of fear were so strong and so uncomfortable. I remember the feeling of closing down into a dark and narrow subjective experience of reality. There was the agitation in the heart, the feeling of being almost nauseous, the tightness in the shoulders, the narrowing of perceptions. For a while it was quite difficult to really stay with the experience—it was more a moment-to-moment struggle between trying to stay present and wanting to escape into comfort. Particularly difficult was the feeling of dread that almost felt like death. But in saying yes to it and being willing to feel the fear with a genuine curiosity, the strong sensations became less intense and less solid.

When we say yes to fear, even though we may feel terror, we

can begin to see there is no real physical danger. We no longer need to panic or try to push it away. As we let it in, we're giving up our fear of fear. We may think we can't stand to feel it, but the truth is we just don't want to. Saying yes to fear is the countermeasure to our resistance; it's the courage to willingly stay present with it. In this example of waiting for my test results, once I was able to truly surrender to the experience, the grip of fear dissolved, and surprisingly, what remained was the experience of genuine equanimity. The dark and closed-down feeling was replaced with sunlight, fresh air, and freedom.

The struggle with fear that I just described was fairly intense and lasted for several days. But it was an excellent learning experience, and the lessons remained. Very recently I received a call from my doctor after what I thought was a routine exam and was told there were signs of a cancerous tumor in my kidney, and that I needed to take another test and prepare to schedule surgery. After my initial shock, I remembered how we are all just one doctor's visit away from falling through the thin ice. And fall I did—right into the icy water! But fairly quickly I remembered to say yes to the arising fears, even while my mind tried to weave the dark and grim story of "Me and My Cancer," along with the corresponding closing down in the body.

Saying yes allowed me to turn away from the story and instead turn toward the understanding that regardless of what might happen, this would be my path to living truly authentically. I actually looked forward to being pushed to work with my deepest attachments—to comfort, to control, to my body, to my future. Saying yes meant I was willing to face all of these things with honesty; that my aspiration to live my life authentically was more important than indulging the story of doom and fear. Remarkably, the episode of falling through the thin ice was very short. It wasn't that all the fear was gone; in truth, there was still anxiety about what would happen. But it didn't predominate, and I was able to see it and relate to it as simply a conditioned response to perceived danger. In other words, there was fear, but I wasn't afraid.

Practice is often described as the willingness to simply be with our life as it is. But this is a difficult concept to get: that practice is not about having a particular state of mind, such as calmness. Nor is it about being completely free of anxiety. This is not to deny that we will, in fact, experience more equanimity, and that our fears will substantially diminish. But, ironically, it's the very demand that life be a particular way that almost guarantees a continuing state of anxiety, unease, and dissatisfaction.

Can you imagine the possibility of having anxiety and not being anxious about it? In other words, not identifying with the story of "I am afraid." This is what happened after I worked with my reaction to the phone call from the doctor. Yet this is certainly not how we usually relate to anxiety and fear. More often, we either try to avoid it or get rid of it. When we feel the disruptive jangle of anxiety, our unspoken thought is that something is wrong, and we might think that being upset is the only possible response. And further, we will almost always feel that something needs to be fixed—that we need to do something to get calm or clear or relaxed.

But consider the possibility of relating to your anxiety in a way where you no longer see it as a problem. For example, if you truly welcome a distressful event with curiosity, as an opportunity to learn, wouldn't that event then become nourishment for your being, rather than poison for the body? In fact, that distressful event pushes you to work with exactly what you need to work with. Let's take a simple example of having to make a phone call where you know the conversation might be unpleasant. Anxiety arises, and the unspoken thought is that something is wrong. We naturally feel the need to get over our anxiety and to calm down. However, from a practice point of view, it doesn't mean it's bad because anxiety arises—all it means is that there is anxiety. It's just a result of our particular conditioning. So we don't have to fight it or make efforts to get rid of it. In fact, instead of viewing it as a problem, we simply pause before making the call, acknowledge the anxiety, then say yes to it—which means we welcome it in as an opportunity to work with the exact place where we are stuck. And then we feel it as the physical experience of our life; we rest in it and learn from it. In other words, we can't necessarily stop having stressful reactions to life at times, but these very reactions, when welcomed and digested with awareness, are transformed into nourishment for our being.

Sometimes we may think we can't say yes. When we find ourselves in the midst of such a painful or distressing experience, usually it is very difficult to stay present with it. This is normal, because as humans, we have a natural aversion to discomfort, and as a consequence our resistance can be very strong. The voice of fear tells us we have reached an edge beyond which we're unwilling to go. Yet our aspiration tells us to take one more step forward. Fear says no!—it warns us to close down and defend. Yet the heart says yes—it calls us to open up and connect. The fundamental point is, until we become intimate with our fears, until we can welcome them, they will always limit our ability to live authentically. Saying yes to life means saying yes to everything, even anxiety and fear. In other words, the path to the truly genuine life requires our openhearted attention to the very things that seem to block our way to it.

However, we also have to acknowledge that sometimes perhaps the experience is too powerful or too overwhelming.

Perhaps it may feel like death itself. After my surgery for kidney cancer this year I had a series of very difficult postoperative complications, including pneumonia, a blood clot in the lungs, and an acute infection—each of which required me to go back into the hospital. I also had some medical procedures that were my worst personal nightmare. One of my blind assumptions that became clear to me afterward was, "None of this was supposed to happen!" Moreover, I was surprised how these events threw me for a loop, even after many years of practice.

Later, in reflecting on these events, I realized how easy it is when we're remembering or writing about our struggles—particularly those that included intense discomfort or uncertainty—to paint a picture in broad brushstrokes by just remembering the highlights. The picture may sound clear and may even be inspiring, but it's almost certain that we're leaving out the many moments when nothing was either clear or inspiring—the moments where we don't know where we stand or what we should do.

I think it's better to paint a more honest picture, for surely, anyone in the midst of intense discomfort and uncertainty has to understand that the bottom line, at least at times, is that things may be very difficult, with no immediate relief in sight. If we expect or assume that we could always overcome these most difficult moments with an intentional practice effort, we may get very discouraged. But that's mainly because we're still holding on to the assumption that practice can handle our difficulties, no matter what they are.

One of the main things I learned is that pain and uncertainty can make us humble. No matter how strong our practice is, these things can still be very difficult. Sometimes our only response may be "Oh shit!"

It's not that I didn't practice. There were many times throughout the day that I would remember to breathe into the chest center and to extend the energy of loving-kindness into the body—simply wishing my body well regardless of how it would all turn out. But this was only possible after I'd regained a modicum of strength; before that, I was basically in survival mode— just getting through the next thing. I think it's important that we don't lose touch with the reality that sometimes we're just in over our heads, and that maybe the best we can do is to simply remember to breathe. This doesn't take away from the value of practice—it just makes the landscape a little more subtle.

In these instances, when discomfort is very strong, or when we're caught in panic or phobias, we may need to first bridge the gap between the old brain, or sympathetic-nervous-system-response of fear, and the cognitive brain, or parasympathetic-nervous-system response, which is somewhat calmer and more amenable to clear thinking. One simple way to bridge this gap is through taking several long, deep breaths—breathing in through the nose and slowly exhaling through the mouth. It may take a little practice, but fairly quickly this can be an effective way to move from the panic response, where practice is not really an option, to a more settled physiological state, where we can then begin to engage with practice.

We may want to then start with only a small step, since the discomfort may still be very strong. We can do a practice called The Three Breaths practice, where we make a deal with the resisting ego by telling it that we will only stay with the discomfort for three breaths, after which point we'll allow ourselves to go off briefly into diversion from the present moment. Paradoxically, the more often we enter into and feel these moments of discomfort, the more we understand that it's more painful to push away the experience than it is to actually feel it. The way we learn this pivotal understanding is "three breaths at a time."

I mentioned that, in my early years in practice, I had the expectation that practice could free me of fear altogether. Now, many years later, it's clear to me that spiritual practice is not so much about being free from anxiety and fear as it is about *not having to* be free from them. There is a subtle but crucial difference between these two understandings. When we can welcome and reside in our anxiety, it's the beginning of bringing the nonjudgmental mind of mercy. We no longer see ourselves as flawed or weak because we have fear—we're able to see it as simply our all-too-human conditioning. We begin to realize that even our most unwanted emotions are simply part of the human condition, and moreover, that they don't have to dominate us. The more deeply we understand what it means to say yes, the less we feel the need to push away fear when it arises. Not having to be free from fear is a gateway to ultimate freedom, and it is what allows us to live most genuinely. We're willing to experience our life—*whatever it is*—and not hide in safety and complacency. The only price we have to pay for this is the risk of exposing ourselves to imagined danger.

13

The Great Teaching

I like to go to the movies, and I particularly like it when I can get to reflect on things in a new way. A while back I saw a documentary called *Protagonist,* about four men who had experienced the fear of powerlessness, and how they each chose strategies to avoid feeling the tremendous discomfort of their fears. Even though each of them went through things that might be very foreign to you or me, their inner experience was not so different.

MARK S.

Mark was a kid who was plagued by fear. He was very small, and always an outcast. The other kids played a game—called "Hit Mark"—where they would throw a ball at him, but he liked it because at least he felt he belonged. Then in junior high they picked on him even more, pushing Hostess fruit pies in his face and soaking him with a squirt gun filled with urine. He remembers having been afraid and hating it—and always feeling powerless.

In high school, after watching a TV series whose hero was a kung fu master, he decided he wanted to have that kind of equanimity, where he could stand up to anyone without fear. His motivation was to smash through his fear and defeat it, so he found a teacher and started taking kung fu lessons. Although this teacher was almost sadistically rough on his students, he had a certainty that seduced Mark, who longed for that kind of certainty. Mark practiced with a fervor that was close to religious obsession and gradually became good at kung fu. He also felt the comfort and power of being part of something bigger.

But he still had the fear of being weak, powerless, and afraid. So he tried to make himself impervious to pain by forcefully going against his fears. He hoped his efforts would give him an instantaneous lightning-bolt transformation, one that would result in calmness and certainty. But in spite of going up against his fears over and over again—doing things such as walking two miles to school in the snow in bare feet—his fear and sense of groundlessness remained. Eventually, he became disillusioned with his sadistic teacher's cruel methods. Discouraged, he turned to marijuana, which seemed at the time to be a much easier way to achieve equanimity, but he soon saw that his pot smoking was just another means of avoidance and escape. Eventually, he managed to find a genuine martial arts teacher, who taught him that kung fu was not about violence and power. When he finally stopped trying to get away from the feeling of powerlessness, he gradually learned that he didn't have to have certainty and control to feel equanimity.

Mark P.

Mark P. was a gay man who was raised in a very religious community. As a youth, when he realized that he might be gay, he was frightened, particularly because in his community homo-sexuality was considered a terrible sin. He did everything possible to avoid his fear of being gay, of being himself. For example, he tried to push sexual thoughts from his mind by reciting lines from the Bible. He eventually became an evangelical preacher, preaching to thousands of people all over the world on the merits of avoiding evil thoughts and acts. But he continued to feel an anxious quiver inside, because his attempts at virtue were primarily a way of trying to get away from himself and from the creeping feeling of groundlessness.

He learned to fast periodically and continued exerting discipline over his thoughts by replacing sexual thoughts with pious ones. He made it his mission to reform other homosexuals, and from this he felt certainty and a sense of power—from the adrenaline rush of preaching to hundreds of converts. Apparently successful at repressing his fears of being gay, he eventually got married and had a child. Still, he would occasionally break out in sweats and trembling—and finally had a breakdown. In the end, his years of repression fell apart, and it became crystal clear to him that he was in fact gay and that this was never going to change.

Yet he was still tortured about what to do about it. When he finally announced publicly that he was gay, his relatives and friends universally rejected him. When he told his young son, his son became very angry with him and cried, asking, "Why can't you be normal?" But when Mark P. also cried and said he'd tried very hard to be different but couldn't change, his son finally understood and said, "It's just like with me—I'm short and no matter how hard I try, I'll always be short." This interaction with his son was instrumental in enabling Mark to fully accept himself. He realized that what we resist will persist, and when he finally accepted himself for who he was and stopped trying to control his fate, he found some peace of mind. He eventually found a male partner and led a normal life as a gay man.

Mark's example may sound extreme, but are our personal strategies that much different? Mark P., like Mark S., was trying to get away from himself, to change himself, and to overcome his feelings of powerlessness and groundlessness. Aren't we all trying to do that to some extent? Mark P. used the discipline of pushing away his thoughts and behavior and relied on the feeling of certainty about the validity of his religious path. It's worth asking ourselves, "Do we have a similar attachment to our own spiritual beliefs and discipline, relying on them to give us a sense of control and certainty?" That kind of certainty solidifies our "story" about who we are and what life is—it gives us a sense of solid ground. Yet all the while we're using our discipline to try to get away from ourselves and our fears, particularly our fear of powerlessness. As with both Mark S. and Mark P., it is good fortune when the inevitable disappointment of following a strategy like this brings us back to the genuine path.

JOE

Joe was a young Mexican man who was also born into a religious home. He remembered his early childhood as being happy and warm. Then, when he was seven, his mother got very sick and died. At that point his father began to beat him mercilessly and repeatedly. Joe was too afraid to fight back and felt powerless, until one day, after his father cracked his ribs and gave him a concussion, Joe took a knife and stabbed his father, almost murdering him. He said this act finally made him feel powerful.

He then took up a life of crime, robbing many banks and enjoying the feeling of power over others that came from holding a gun. Often he would feel panic before the robberies, but then he would conjure up memories of his childhood abuse to reignite his rage, and that would give him the feeling of power he needed and some temporary solace from his panic and fear. He felt high on his life of crime and also a sense of certainty in what he was doing—just the opposite of the powerlessness he was running away from. He said he wanted to be an Übermensch—a superman—and even when he was eventually caught and put in prison, he joined the toughest gang. Then, at one point, he was put into solitary confinement for two years. The darkness and isolation broke through his false veneer of power, and he lost all sense of solid ground. His ego fragmented, and he literally fell apart, realizing that he was not an Übermensch at all but instead a person who was very frightened and vulnerable.

After this he could no longer go back to his strategy of violence, and he began reflecting on his childhood, remembering that he had once been innocent and gentle. In order to heal his rage, he began to write about his life. Eventually, when he got out of prison, he became a journalist and tried to atone for the remorse he felt at hurting others, such as the female teller who'd been so afraid when he held up the bank where she was working that she peed on herself. He finally realized that the false certainty he'd once felt had prevented him from experiencing real humility, and from this experience of groundlessness he eventually found genuine peace of mind.

Joe didn't have an awareness practice as we know it, but he had the good fortune of being able to learn from his disappointment, particularly from his ordeal in solitary confinement, which had fragmented and dismantled his false stance of power. Sometimes we have to be forced to surrender to the great teaching of the helplessness of the loss of control—something we'd never do willingly.

HANS

Hans was a German political activist. His mother, who was Jewish and had been in a concentration camp, killed herself when he was an infant. As a result, he was raised by foster parents and remembered having had a happy childhood until he was nine. However, at that point, whenever he'd see his father, who was a policeman and an anti-Semite, his father would beat him. Then one day he saw policemen beating a women and her children, and his whole idealized image of his father and of the police as protectors fell apart. At that point he became a political activist, trying to right the wrongs he witnessed during the 1970s. He said that Germans had ignored the evil of Hitler and shouldn't continue to ignore present-day evils. He felt he had to do something to overcome his feeling of powerlessness. Gradually he became more and more active, and more and more violent. When one of his fellow activists died in prison, he became intoxicated with rage. He became a terrorist, a guerilla, and rose high in the ranks. He became a colleague of Carlos the Jackal, perhaps the world's most famous terrorist before Osama bin Laden. Hans said that when he held a gun in his hands, he no longer felt powerless; instead he felt like he ruled heaven and earth.

Then one day, during a violent kidnapping attempt, three innocent people were shot and killed, and he, too, was shot. Although he was considered a hero by his friends, he experienced tremendous remorse for what he was doing. He realized that he was becoming worse than those he opposed, that all his ideals had turned upside down, and that he felt truly groundless. Once drunk on power and certainty, he now felt devastated by the consequences of his actions. He went into hiding, chased by both the police and the terrorists; but out of remorse for what he had done, he wrote to the newspapers, divulging future terrorist plots. After twenty-five years in hiding he was caught and went to prison, but by then he was a changed man. He experienced tremendous remorse for the suffering he had caused, seeing through his prior certainty for the sham it was—a dodge to avoid his own feelings of powerlessness. As a result of his experience of groundlessness and his remorse for what he had done, he was able to make sincere efforts to live more honestly and genuinely.

Each of these four men had his own unique journey, but we can notice our own parallel tendencies. When we don't like who we are and make efforts to try to change ourselves, are we really different from these four men? We, too, have an aversion to feeling a lack of control, and we, too, choose strategies that give us a false sense of power and certainty. Although these four men's lives may seem very different from ours, recent world events continue to remind us how precarious life is for all of us. Normally we're so insulated, maintaining such a narrow view of things, that we glide through life on automatic pilot, ignoring the sense of how thin the ice beneath us really is. Like these four men, we try to avoid the anxious quiver inside of us by manipulating our world to make it feel safe, secure, and comfortable. We particularly want to avoid the feelings of groundlessness, uncertainty, and loss of control.

It's very difficult for us to accept the reality that life is not subject to our control—that it is always changing. Much of our suffering arises when we resist this reality. The inherent groundlessness of life as it is—of the changing and impermanent nature of things—makes us feel very uncomfortable. Thus we try mightily to put ground under our feet. We pretend we're in control, in the same way that the steersman in a rowboat thinks he's in control of his boat. He moves his rudder and to some extent he can determine where his boat will go. But he forgets that the stream is going at its own speed and that there may well be unknown twists and turns and rapids ahead. Like him, we may occasionally realize that we're not in control, but as soon as our boat hits the quiet waters, we fall back into the illusion that we can control what happens. We simply don't want to feel the uncertainty and groundlessness that this illusion attempts to cover over.

But when the external world seems like it's falling apart, such as with the threat of global financial instability, mass shootings, or the seeming inability of government to address critical issues such as genocide, world hunger, global warming, or even the budget—it can feel as if we've fallen right into the icy water, with little control over events in our life. It's easy to feel lost and groundless in these times, and we may not see how our spiritual practice can be quite relevant. Hopefully we understand that it's not worthwhile to indulge in anger or blame, or to wring our hands over the horrible state of things. Yet dense and intense emotional reactions can leave us feeling lost and overwhelmed. Talking with others or taking some kind of action may seem to relieve our distress, but despite any valuable function this may serve, it can also act as a cover-up, keeping us from feeling what none of us wants to feel—the helplessness of the loss of control.

The sense of helplessness is no doubt one of our biggest fears, but this is not something new. Haven't we always been just one doctor's visit away from falling through the thin ice? Acute current events simply bring this fact to the surface, that the world around us is unpredictable and precarious. There are also times when our personal emotional distress is particularly powerful, such as when we're struck with serious illness, chronic pain, a relationship crisis, or financial and work reversals. At these times, it can seem as if meditation techniques such as observing the mind or feeling the spaciousness of the breath aren't quite enough to deal with the churning anxiety that we're experiencing.

When it seems as if the future is dissolving right in front of us, we need to know how to practice with the experience of uncertainty; otherwise we'll remain confused and anxious, and we will continue to detour away from genuine equanimity into the artificial comfort of distractions, busyness, or efforts to control our world. When we experience the discomfort of groundlessness, and especially the feeling of panic when things go really awry, our little mind will naturally resist. It will tell us to fix it right now or to find a sense of ground or some escape. But practice asks us to view the discomfort, even the panic, with a curiosity that's willing to explore exactly what we're feeling in the present moment. This is what it means to say yes—to simply want to know *what* our life is, whether it's interesting or boring, pleasant or unpleasant, joyful or painful.

What helps us open to the experience of a life that no longer fits our expectations—where safety, security, and certainty are no longer givens, where what we counted on is gone, and where there may be little left for us to hold on to? It starts with a question: How do we actually work with this sinking feeling of anxiety, of having no ground? Do we understand what it means to surrender to the insecurity of groundlessness itself? Can we get out of our heads, with our stories about ourselves and our plight, and instead open our eyes and hearts and finally face the fears we've never wanted to face?

Perhaps we should first ask, "What does it actually mean to surrender?" Surrender means, very specifically, to cease fighting—to give up. But give up what? First, give up our resistance, including our constant effort to avoid discomfort. Surrender also requires that we give up our stories, such as our stories about how our life should be comfortable or within our control, or our stories about how awful things are—stories that are invariably about "Me" and "Mine." Surrender ultimately means giving ourselves up completely to what is.

But the fact is we can't force ourselves to surrender. We can't just drop our resistance simply because we want to. What we *can* do, however, is experience *the totality of what we are in this very moment.* We can focus all of our attention on the exact truth of our own mental, emotional, and physical experience, which includes our resistance. To do this includes acknowledging the detours that we often take—our self-deceptions, our craving to escape, our blaming—because these things separate us from reality, as well as increasing our bodily tension. The practice of surrender means feeling the totality of this with an unwavering intensity, allowing the cocoon that protects us, the hard shell that covers the heart, to begin to break open. When we can enter into this dark place fully, something else emerges. Tibetan Buddhist meditation teacher Pema Chödrön wrote, "Only to the extent that we expose ourselves over and over to annihilation can that which is indestructible in us be found." The grace that can flow from consciously experiencing our pain becomes a gift that transcends our imagined helplessness.

The specific practice is to move toward, and to fully reside in the physicality of our discomfort, allowing the fear, the sadness, the grief, to be breathed directly into the center of the chest. In the darkest circumstances, breathing into the heart is the one thing that will always be a genuine response to the moment. Using the breath as a conduit, it's *as if* we're breathing the swirling physical sensations and energy of distress right into the chest center. Then, on the outbreath, we simply exhale. We're not trying to alter our experience; we're simply using the heart's breath as a container to fully feel our distress. We can also include the wider sense of the breath—the air all around us—which gives us a bigger context for experiencing whatever is present.

The process of surrender is to take all of it in—the distress, the resistance, the protections, the breath into the heart, the environment—and to feel it all fully.

In other words, it's to experience the totality of what we are in this very moment. It is here that we can come to understand the paradox that the experience of real ground comes from surrendering to groundlessness itself. We can experience the rock-bottom security that grows out of opening into our deepest doubts and insecurities. It is also here that the sweetness of the simple joy of Being becomes available to us.

I recently had a six-month roller coaster ride that started with getting a kidney cancer diagnosis and ended with having surgery and a long and difficult recovery. First there was the anxiety and uncertainty about what would happen. Then, after being told that the tumor had to be cut out, I began exploring other options, including doing a less-risky procedure. But fairly quickly these other options were put in doubt. Anyone who has been through the process with the medical establishment knows there are no easy answers as to what to do, with risks connected to every choice.

It was impossible for me to find any certainty, so my path was to surrender to the experience of uncertainty as best I could, while at the same time objectively researching my best options. I eventually canceled the original surgery and opted for another form of surgery, in which they would attempt to freeze the tumor to death rather than cutting it out. But even then it was hard to choose a surgeon—there was never any certainty that I was making the right choice. The uncertainty continued well after the surgery, with a variety of postoperative complications that I described in the previous chapter. All of this was quite challenging, but also, in the end, very rewarding. In fact, one of the unexpected benefits was my opening into a bigger sense of compassion for others. Letting our uncertainty be breathed into the heart seems to cultivate compassion, since we are opening to the shared pain of being human—the shared pain that anyone with health issues has to go through. However, to experience the depth of compassion we have to first experience the depth of our own struggle, which, in turn, is the touch point to connecting with the universal pain of being human.

The point is that the path of the authentic life requires being open to change, to the unknown, to *whatever* arises. Prioritizing safety and control guarantees that our life will remain both very small and very unsatisfying. Yes, we fear change and discomfort, and we prefer the quiet waters; but in order to live more genuinely, we need be more wary of our desire for comfort and complacency than we are of our fear of change. We can learn that in those moments when our expectations and plans crumble and there seems to be nothing left, it is only by completely surrendering to what is that we can realize that what remains is more than enough. This is what the four men in the movie learned, each in his own way. When we reach our lowest moments, a part of us gets exposed that we're rarely in touch with when things are going well, and when we enter into it consciously, this is the very part that opens the door to the essence of our existence. Surrendering to the physical reality of the present moment, we learn to go deeper with each in-breath, entering the silence, the equanimity, of reality-as-it-is. The experience of groundlessness transforms from our worst fear to the Great Teaching, because it forces us to give up our deepest attachments and surrender to what is.

14

What We Really Want

I recently read a book called *The Long Walk*—the supposedly true and compelling story of a small group of people dealing with extreme adversity. Their quest was to find freedom—not freedom from their emotions and attachments, but literal freedom—from being imprisoned without just cause. At the time of the story, around 1939, the author, Slavomir Rawicz, was twenty-five years old. He was a lieutenant in the Polish army, and with no warning was arrested by the Russians for being a spy. He was taken from his new wife, whom he never saw again, and was arbitrarily imprisoned. We have often returned to the theme of how we're all skating on thin ice, and how easily and without warning we can fall through it. What happened to Slav was a perfect example, for not only was there no warning, there was no legitimate reason for his arrest. Yet his life as he knew it changed forever, and in ways he could never have imagined.

For his first few months in jail he was tortured every day. They asked him to sign a confession saying that he was a spy, but his sense of honor, as well as his stubbornness and pride, wouldn't allow him to sign it, even though he expected to be killed for not signing. For days on end he was placed upright in a narrow box, like a vertical coffin, and allowed out only for hours of beatings and interrogations. Finally, after months of torture they held a mock trial and sentenced him to twenty-five years of hard labor in a Siberian prison camp.

The journey across Russia, from Moscow to Siberia, sounds similar to how the Nazis transported the Jews in cattle cars to the concentration camps. The Russian prisoners were given no food or water for days on end and they had to stand upright, elbow to elbow, urinating and defecating where they stood. Many froze to death or died from illness. After they got off the trains, they were all chained together, two abreast, and had to walk for weeks through freezing snow and blizzards. They were given a cup of coffee and a hunk of bread each day, and when one of them would get weak and fall down, they would be un-chained and left to freeze to death.

When they finally got to the Siberian labor camp, which was just a few hundred miles south of the Artic Circle, Slav immedi-ately decided to try to escape. He was young and still strong, and was determined not to spend his next twenty-five years in the prison camp. Gradually he found six other inmates who were willing to attempt the seemingly impossible task of escaping. They prepared as best they could, hoarding food and gathering clothing to keep warm. The author describes the escape and their long walk south, first through the Siberian wilderness, then through Mongolia, across the Gobi Desert, and finally across the Himalayas. When they arrived in India, they finally felt that they were free.

The details of their long walk are compelling. They walked for eighteen months straight, across three thousand miles of some of the most difficult terrain in the world, through freezing blizzards, crossing many turbulent rivers, through scorching desert heat—often going for days without food or water. What struck me most was their absolute determination to survive. Every day one of them would say the words "Let's go," and they would all begin walking again. There was very little complaining or dramatizing, and although they certainly felt the fear of not surviving, they didn't let it get in the way of their resolute perseverance to make it to freedom.

It's interesting to look at our own desire to be free in light of what these men had to endure. There's a relevant line from another of my favorite books—*Lying Awake* by Mark Salzman: "No matter how many times we hear what it costs to practice, we're still shocked when the bill comes, and we wonder all over again if we can pay it." Yet, in reading about their encounters with one difficulty after another, I was definitely inspired by their perseverance—their ability to keep going, no matter how much they were hurting or how they felt emotionally. This does not mean they were "practicing" in the way we might understand it—they were probably going on pure survival instinct. But their ability to keep putting one foot in front of the other is vaguely analogous to our taking one more conscious breath to stay present, even when everything in us is telling us to turn away.

I'm close to seventy years old, and in recent months I've had many recollections of my ten years as a hospice volunteer, which began in the early nineties when I was forty-eight. One particular memory was of my second hospice patient, who himself was close to seventy at the time and still an active horseshoer in Northern California, when out of the blue he was diagnosed with liver cancer. He died four months later, and what happened to him is another perfect example of how we're all skating on thin ice. The Buddha exhorted us to remember that we are not here forever; he said we should remind ourselves that each day could be our last. The truth is, we have no idea how long we have, yet we unconsciously assume we have endless time. But if we remember that we have limited time, we can begin to understand that each day is precious and that we waste much of our life replaying the past and worrying about the future. We can begin, perhaps for the first time, to take our life seriously. We can also begin to truly appreciate the people around us—the fact that they, too, have limited time. Do we want to continue our self-centered and small-minded behaviors toward others, when any one of us could die at any time? We certainly wouldn't want someone to die while we were angry at them or filled with petty thoughts and judgments about them.

The ephemeral nature of our lives reminds us to bring a little more urgency to really being here, to committing more fully to our spiritual path. This urgency doesn't need to be grim—we can be serious in our purpose without being morose.

There's an old Zen term called *tangaryo*. It's used to describe the five-day sitting period that new students go through to demonstrate their sincerity before being allowed to enter the monastery. But the deeper meaning is that it is a time of looking at ourselves as if we were examining a leaf, seeing every detail in depth, looking at what we understand, what we value, and the depth of our commitments.

A particularly interesting question to ask ourselves is, "What am I *truly* committed to?" It's especially important to see how many of our "Me's" are committed to "sleep": the Me that believes its thoughts and judgments, the Me that is ruled by its emotions, the Me that can't stay present for more than few moments. The Dalai Lama had an interesting comment on the fact that we are committed to waking sleep. When asked what surprises him most, he answered it was man. He said man sacrifices his health in order to make money. Then he sacrifices money to recuperate his health. And then he is so anxious about the future that he does not enjoy the present. As a result, he does not live in the present or the future; he lives as if he is never going to die and then dies having never really lived.

It's important to understand that what we really want—what we're committed to—is defined precisely by what we actually do. For example, if we spend a lot of time mindlessly surfing the Web, that means we're committed to entertaining ourselves with diversions. If we expend a lot of our energy in anger or worry, it means we're committed to reinforcing those exact emotional patterns. We can say and believe that our deepest commitment is to waking up and living authentically, but a verbal commitment is not enough. Our commitment has to be manifested in how we live and in the depth of our ability to persevere.

This is why it's so important to be honest in observing how we spend our time and energy. This isn't about making ourselves feel guilty, but rather to see clearly where we choose to be "asleep." At some point we may begin to feel remorse for what we're actually committed to, and this, in turn, can help us to cultivate new commitments. For example, if we're committed to being angry, or worrying, or wasting time online—at some point we may need to feel the remorse of being disconnected from our true heart before we can truly commit to living more genuinely. When I speak about remorse, I'm not referring to guilt. Guilt is based in thinking—it is anger directed against ourselves for things we've done. Remorse is based in the heart—it is the ache in the heart that arises when we go against our true nature.

Please be clear that we can have many healthy commitments—to people, to our work, to physical activities. These commitments can certainly contribute to a sense of personal happiness, where we feel a sense of fulfillment. The commitment to living authentically is a little different, in that the essential qualities we're cultivating—such as the ability to be present, to live openly and honestly, to live from gratitude and with kindness—bring a much deeper level of happiness. The more we are committed to living genuinely, which on the most profound level is what we really want, the more our priorities become clear.

I heard a relevant story recently. A Zen teacher stood before his students with a very large and empty glass jar. He wordlessly picked up some round stones around the size of small plums and proceeded to fill the jar with them. He then asked the students if the jar was full. They agreed that it was. The teacher then picked up a box of pebbles and poured them into the jar. He shook the jar lightly. The pebbles rolled into the open areas between the stones. He then asked the students again if the jar was full. They said yes. Next the teacher picked up a box of sand and poured it into the jar. Of course, the sand filled up everything else. He asked once more if the jar was full. The students unanimously agreed. The teacher then produced a glass of water and poured the entire contents into the jar, effectively filling the empty space between the sand. The students laughed. "Now," said the teacher, "I want you to recognize that this jar represents your life. The stones are the important things—the aspiration to realize your true nature, the wish to live more authentically, the perseverance and commitment to cultivate presence, gratitude, and kindness—and if everything else was lost and only they remained, your life would still be full. The pebbles are the other things that matter, such as your health, your friends, and perhaps your job. The sand is everything else—the small stuff, including your house, your car, your possessions. If you put the sand into the jar first, there is no room for the stones or the pebbles. The same goes for life. If you spend all your time and energy on the small stuff, you will never have room for the things that are important to you. Pay attention to the things that are critical to your genuine happiness. Take care of the things that really matter first. Set your priorities. The rest is just sand." One of the students raised her hand and inquired what the water represented. The teacher smiled and said, "I'm glad you asked. The water just shows you that no matter how full your life may seem, there's always room for a little more practice, to make your life even fuller."

One of the ways we can remember our priorities is to invoke the question of the eternal recurrence. When we reach a choice point, where we can do either something that reinforces complacency and waking sleep or something that helps us live more authentically, we can ask, "If I had to live my life over again and again and again, in the exact same way, throughout eternity, what would I do right now?" Sometimes I wake up in the middle of the night and can't go back to sleep. There's a desire to drift off into daydreams and fantasies to avoid feeling the discomfort that I'm feeling, but when I ask the question of the eternal recurrence, the answer is always clear: what I most genuinely wish to do is dwell in the heart of awareness. When I remember this, I simply breathe into the center of the chest, saying the following lines:

Breathing in, dwelling in the heart;
Breathing out, just being.

The key point is that if we don't live according to what we genuinely value, we lose our life—moment by moment.

One last point about commitment: one of the essential aspects of commitment is the quality of perseverance. Perseverance is what allowed Slav and his companions to carry on in the face of sometimes daunting and seemingly hopeless circumstances. Their commitment to survive and free themselves from being enslaved was what drove them, and perseverance enabled them not to succumb to their impulses toward safety or comfort. If they had indulged those impulses, they almost certainly would have failed in their quest. The same is true for us: once we understand what we really want, the only way to carry through on this commitment is to persevere through all of the moments when the mind tells us to turn away or to give up.

There is a practice aphorism that is particularly relevant to the quality of perseverance:

Strength exercised equals more strength.
Weakness indulged equals more weakness.

Definitions are important here: By "strength" we mean determination, perseverance, knowing our values and priorities. By "weakness" we mean defaulting into distractions, passivity, and self-indulgence. In short, this is another way of saying we get good at what we practice. For example, the more we sit in meditation, or attend retreats, the stronger our ability to be present. Likewise, when we allow ourselves to regularly miss meditation, it becomes much more difficult to maintain the ability to really be here. Once we establish our commitment, we can see how that commitment grows as we persevere.

The more we make efforts to live authentically, the deeper is our understanding that our purpose is to know who we truly are. And as we connect with ourselves, with our own hearts, we also begin to tap into our interconnection with others. There's a poignant example of this implicit understanding in *The Long Walk*. The men on the journey were different nationalities and ages and didn't know each other well when they started out. But the shared hardships formed a bond of camaraderie that allowed them to get through their struggles. On one occasion, when they were near the top of the Himalayan peaks, it was so cold that they had to stay awake all night to avoid freezing to death in their sleep. So the four remaining members—three of them had already died—stood together, arm in arm, continuously waking one another up. This is a great reminder of how helpful it can be to travel the spiritual path with like-minded people, where the sense of connection with others can help us to persevere and maintain our commitment to waking up.

15

Sound Bites That Matter

"Not Happening Now!"

A few decades ago the phrase "Be here now" was one of the most popular phrases in practice. It was not only popular, it also contained a very pointed and succinct message that goes to the essence of what practice is about. An equally powerful, although slightly more subtle message is "Not happening now!" Instead of focusing on being present, the emphasis is on uncovering how much mental spinning we're adding and how it obscures the reality of the present moment.

This obscuring mental spinning is particularly obvious when we're emotionally distressed. In fact, much of our distress comes from the negative thoughts that we add to whatever is actually happening. For example, when we get sick, it's very common to begin weaving negative imaginings about the future. An extreme example is when we have a bad headache and begin imagining we have a brain tumor. It's also easy to get caught in future-think when we have a financial setback with attendant scenarios of doom. The antidote is to say, "Not happening now!" This phrase is a reminder that most of what is causing us anxiety in the present moment is only happening in our mind.

When we say the phrase, we can follow it by asking, "What am I adding?" This question points us directly to thoughts such as "I can't do this," which is based on a negative self-image; or "I shouldn't have to go through this," which is rooted in a sense of entitlement; or "It's his fault," which is based on being caught in stories about the past. In each of these examples we're adding a mental spin to what is happening, In fact, in almost every example of our emotional distress, what we're adding to the present moment is either from the past or from an imagined future, and in each case it makes the situation worse.

"Not happening now!" has become one of my favorite practice phrases, primarily because it is so direct—it cuts right through a lot of our mental confusion. Sometimes, when I'm sitting in meditation, if I become aware that I'm imagining a difficult conversation with someone, all I have to do is say, "Not happening now!" and it's like poking a pin in a balloon—it just disappears. There may still be a residue of anxiety or anger or sadness to deal with, but without the added mental spin, any emotion that is there can be experienced more directly. In other words, this phrase allows us to drop the stories and actually be here now—to come back to what is *actually* happening now, such as breathing, the bodily experience, or awareness of the environment.

This phrase has been particularly helpful to me of late. When my mind started weaving scenarios of worry or doom about an upcoming surgery for kidney cancer, I had to learn where the line was between "Not happening now!" and thinking about what I needed to do on an objective level. For example, when I was trying to choose what kind of surgery I wanted to have, I had to consider the different risks involved in the four choices. In such cases, it's easy to jump into negative imaginings about what would happen if the risks became realities—such as losing my whole kidney, or worse. So it was important not to get caught up in the imaginings while I was trying to objectively evaluate what to do. Of course, in making decisions, it's always partly a crapshoot, but when we don't get lost in excessive thinking, we can at least be clearer in our choices. "Not happening now!" has allowed me to maintain a degree of clarity and sanity and avoid getting caught up in the stories the little mind seems intent on weaving.

Don't Go There!

"Don't go there!" is a phrase that may not need to be used very often, but when we're caught in obsessive thinking, it is perhaps the best phrase to cut through our addictive thought patterns. When we're feeling emotional distress, our minds can become fixated in thought loops, especially if we've been criticized or feel threatened. Thoughts of blame and self-justification, which are defenses against a perceived attack, can become relentless. When caught in this addictive cycle, it can be very difficult to get out. Even if we sit down to meditate, the mind is most likely to continue in the compulsion to blame and self-justify. Just following the breath, or other tried-and-true meditation techniques, don't seem strong enough to break the addictive cycle of thinking.

The one tool that I've found to be effective in these situations is to say the phrase "Don't go there!" The instruction is to say the phrase every single time the obsessive thinking begins.

Over and over again: "Don't go there!" and then return to present-moment awareness. It's as if we're wielding a sword, cutting off the thoughts each and every time they arise. If we do this consistently, after a while the addictive cycle will be broken. It's similar to tending a fire: each time we put a log on the fire, it burns hotter, but as we stop feeding the fire, it will eventually go out. Saying, "Don't go there!" is a way of putting out the mental fire; we're depriving the mind of the fuel that comes with each thought.

Normally, our practice is not to oppose our thoughts or try to stop them, because trying to stop our thoughts or feelings can easily lead to suppression. Rather, our basic practice is to be open to whatever arises and to observe it with curiosity. But when we're caught in obsessive thinking, sometimes we have to shift gears. However, as soon as the mind cools down, we drop the practice of saying, "Don't go there!" and return to simply observing the mind. This is a good example of the fact that practice can never be reduced to a formula. It is much more an art form, and how we apply that art is based on an increasing refinement of how we understand the subtleties of what is going on in the present moment.

"How Is It Supposed to Be?"

This question is pivotal to clarifying where we're caught in unconscious expectations. Often when we're experiencing emotional distress, there are deeply believed thoughts on board of which we're not aware. Some of these thoughts are in the form of assumptions and expectations that are so much a part of our mental makeup that we are literally blind to them.

Asking "How is it supposed to be?" is similar to asking the basic practice question "What is my most believed thought?"

But it differs in being more directed and specific. It asks us to question our particular expectation in a particular situation. For example, if we are angry at how we are being treated but still somewhat confused about what we're feeling, asking "How is it supposed to be?" can point us directly to the expectation/belief "People should appreciate me." This discovery will allow us to move more quickly from the surface reaction of anger to the underlying hurt that was previously not recognized. Once we're aware of the thought component of our emotional reaction (our expectation), we will be less likely to get caught up in the story of anger and blame and more able to be present with our experience. As long as the story line is running, it is extremely difficult to extricate ourselves from our emotional reactions, because the story keeps the emotion locked in place.

Asking "How is it supposed to be?" can become even more directed when dealing with relationship issues. For example, the question can be refined to, "How is he/she supposed to be?" We always have expectations of how people are supposed to be. This is true even in our closest relationships, and often we're totally unaware of what these expectations are. Yet whenever we have an emotional reaction, we can be sure that we're reacting, at least in part, from our unfulfilled expectations. For example, we expect others to be appreciative, kind, supportive, attentive, affectionate, and on and on. Then, when we don't get what we want, we react with disappointment, and until we uncover the source of this disappointment, we will fester in anger or resentment.

Interestingly, as we clarify our expectations of others in relationships, we can go even deeper and uncover our own hidden agendas, by asking, "How am *I* supposed to be?" Every time we have an expectation of how another person is supposed to be, it is rooted in an expectation of how *we* would like to feel. For example, we may want someone to be supportive so that we can feel secure. Or we want someone to be attentive so that we can feel that we count. Or we want someone to be affectionate so that we can feel loved. Surprisingly, we're often unaware of our most basic motivations. But asking the question is a direct and very specific way of clarifying where we're caught in our own blind agendas.

REFRAIN FROM BLAMING

One of the stickiest areas of spiritual practice is relationships, and the single most important precept in working through relationship issues is "Refrain from blaming." When our expectations aren't met and we experience disappointment, instead of looking inward, we will often focus on blaming the other person. Blaming is very seductive, since it gives us a feeling of control and power. This is reinforced by the feeling of certitude, the feeling of being right, which explains why blaming is such a common pattern. Yet being caught in this pattern is the essence of living inauthentically—believing our stories and identifying with the smallest part of ourselves.

Refraining from blaming is very difficult, in part because we love the juicy feeling of being right. Perhaps equally important, blaming allows us to avoid experiencing the feelings that we don't want to feel, such as hurt, sadness, and fear. When we are disappointed in our relationships, these deeper feelings will automatically be triggered—the fear of being unworthy, the fear of being alone, the fear of rejection, the fear of being hurt again, the fear of being controlled, or the fear of the loss of safety. We have a natural aversion to feeling these fears, so we automatically move into blaming. When blaming takes over, the feelings are pushed down out of awareness, where we don't have to feel them.

When we understand this whole dynamic, of how blaming allows us to avoid dealing with what's truly going on, we are more motivated to follow the pivotal dictate "Refrain from blaming." Sometimes, when the impulse to blame is particularly strong, we may first have to invoke the instruction "Don't go there!" This will allow us to break the cycle of addictive thinking that often accompanies self-righteousness and blaming. When I work with students who are caught in blaming, I strongly discourage them from focusing on the other person. The teaching is to keep coming back to one's own experience, to allow ourselves to feel the hurt and fear that are so often right under the hard protective veneer of blaming. What's interesting is that when we can refrain from blaming and from being right, we will often discover what part we ourselves have played in the relationship difficulty. The more honest we are in being present with our own experience, the more we will realize that no one is totally blameless.

"Become Present as Often as Possible" and "Remain Present as Long as Possible"

Being present is the essence of what it means to wake up and live authentically. This phrase reminds us how important it is to make efforts to be present, not just when we're meditating but throughout the day as well. It also reminds us how important the quality of perseverance is—the ability to make efforts to be aware, regardless of how we're feeling in the moment and regardless of the success of our efforts. Only with perseverance can we overcome the inevitable forces of resistance.

In order to become present as often as possible, it's helpful to understand what, specifically, we're being present to; otherwise, this aphorism will be too general to be of actual use. First, we become present to the breath and the body, which means to physically feel the specific sensations involved in breathing, as well as the sensations and energy throughout the body. Second, we become present to our mind and our emotions, which means knowing, specifically, what we're thinking and believing, and also knowing what we're feeling emotionally. This includes actually *feeling* our emotions in the body. Third, we become present to the environment around us—to whatever is outside of the skin boundary, such as sounds, air, light, and so on. Being present to the environment is particularly important in helping us get beyond the narrow sense of being a separate "Me." Last, we become present to a gestalt sense of the moment, where the whole of our experience is more than the sum of our sensations, thoughts, and emotions.

Becoming present as often as possible does not require that we be sitting in meditation. We can take many brief "pauses in time" throughout the day, where we may wake up to reality for just a few breaths at a time. We can be driving, walking, sitting at our desk, cooking, or even having a conversation with someone. Some people set an alarm on their watch to go off periodically to wake them up to the moment. Others place Post-its in conspicuous places. The point is that we do whatever we have to, even in small doses, to become present as often as possible.

Part of being present for as long as possible requires continuing to study what gets in the way of being awake. We have to observe all of our ways of resisting the present moment, including all of our detours and escapes, such as analyzing, judging, blaming, and our endless diversions. As we observe this process—

the struggle between the "Yes, I want to be present" and the "No, I want to stay asleep"—the scales gradually begin to tip from the no to the yes, and our ability to stay present becomes more natural. The longer we can stay present, the more we're able to experience an authentic life of genuine happiness.

PART FOUR

Awakening the Heart

16

The Bigger Picture

I once heard a dying man ask, "What is the point of this miserable life?" The question itself reflects the unfortunate consequences of seeing life as miserable. A major problem for most of us, in life as well as in practice, is that our view is so myopic, so shortsighted, that we miss the bigger point. On the animal level, the point is simply to live, to survive. Beyond survival, however, the bigger point is to live as authentically as possible. Why? Because it's our nature to do so. Our true nature strives to reveal itself, like an acorn strives to become an oak. This is why our deepest satisfaction is to become who we truly are.

However, we usually go from one thing to another, often only seeing what's right in front of us. Much of the day we're lost in or identified with whatever we're doing, rather than being actually aware of who we are and what we're doing with our life. And often, what we focus on is based primarily on wanting to be comfortable or secure in some way. We can spend a lot of our energy trying to fortify a particular self-image, such as being nice, or competent, or helpful. We spend still more time and energy following our usual strategies, such as trying to please others in order to gain approval, or trying to prove our worth, or trying to gain control to ward off chaos. These strategies are always based in fear, and when we devote our energy to fortifying these self-images and pursuing our usual strategies, that energy isn't available for what helps us live more authentically, more awake.

What I'm describing, of course, is the basic human predicament—that in striving to be comfortable and secure, we are cut off from awareness of our true nature. In contrast to this, it's possible to have a particular experience of presence and a clearer sense of who we really are and what our life is actually about. But what's remarkable is how seldom this experience occurs; and as a consequence, our life stays very small and, most often, perplexing to us. The question, "What is this life really about?" may sound philosophical, but unless we ask this question over and over, unless we look beyond what makes us comfortable and secure, our life will never be genuine or deeply satisfying. Exploring what our life is really about is not the same as analyzing it or trying to get a mental handle on it. Of course, we all try to do that in our own way, as a means of maintaining control. But it should be obvious that no matter what we do to try to control our life, we can't make things turn out exactly the way we want. This doesn't mean we shouldn't try to have some control, or take responsibility, or make plans, such as toward getting a degree, preparing to have a family, saving to buy a house, planning for retirement, and so on. These are all reasonable pursuits. Yet we can be involved in these types of plans and still have a very myopic view, based mainly on the narrow and self-centered desire to primarily be comfortable and secure.

Without a bigger view of what life is we will continue to sleepwalk through life without a sense of conscious purpose. We have to ask ourselves, within our everyday plans, "Is there a bigger view?" Is there an understanding of what our life is really about? Is there a sense of purpose beyond just career, family, and retirement? In other words, is there a genuine commitment to an authentic life of awakening?

I remember one day sitting on the beach when I was in my midtwenties. I was watching some seagulls, and the question occurred to me whether or not we are really any different from the seagulls, who are born, live their seagull life of flying, eating, reproducing . . . and then they die. On one level, it is clear that we aren't any different; the physical body is born, it lives, and then it dies. On a different level, many teachers say that "life" and "death" are just concepts, and that who we truly are—the interconnectedness of all and everything—never dies, but only changes form. Although this may be true, it does not negate the level of everyday reality, where it is so crucial that we understand that we don't have endless time.

To get a sense of this, it's worthwhile to take the time to go out on a clear night and look up at the stars. Astronomers tell us that at best we can see about two thousand stars; yet in our galaxy alone there are 400 billion stars. What's even more amazing is that our galaxy is only one of 400 billion galaxies! When we observe the immensity of the cosmos, we can readily understand that life is much vaster than we ever imagined. We may even have the good fortune to occasionally experience a taste of the vastness, the mystery. These tastes give us direct knowledge that we are more than just our little "Me"—that, as Shakespeare said, "There is more to life than is dreamt of in your philosophy." Even if the sense of our interconnectedness with all of life is only vague, it still gives us an experiential taste of a bigger view of reality.

Yet it is very easy to forget and lose sight of the bigger view.

Suzuki Roshi once said, "The most important thing . . . is to find out . . . what is the most important thing." When we don't remember this, we end up protecting ourselves, wasting time on unnecessary things, and staying caught in complacency. One way to viscerally remind ourselves of the bigger view is to simply pause, take a long, slow breath, and feel the air enter the body. Then be aware that the air you take in is the same air that is all around you and that, on the exhale, the air inside of you becomes the air outside. We can immediately tap into a taste of the interconnectedness that we are, even if it's on a very small scale. As a pointer to look deeper, it's important to understand, even conceptually, that we *are* the air we breathe as well as the ground that we walk on. Just as we each share this air and this ground, we share in the life energy that courses through each living thing. Reality on this level is vast. To realize our true nature of connectedness means we understand, experientially, that we *are* the vastness, and also, at any given moment, a unique manifestation of it.

It's good to consider how often we're in touch with a sense of this bigger view of life—a view that at least has waking up as the central orientation. It's particularly worth asking, "How do we understand the bigger view in terms of what we're actually doing in practice?" When I started practicing, I was heavily influenced by the book *The Three Pillars of Zen,* in which the idea of enlightenment was one of the main themes. Many of us who read this were left with the idea that we had to *try* to become enlightened—meaning that through our hard efforts we would have a miraculous breakthrough out of our normal way of perceiving reality, and achieve a permanent change in our state of being. This was the bigger view for me and many others at that time: enlightenment was seen as a state that would relieve us of all anxiety and distress, and moreover, that it would be a

permanent state of wisdom and freedom. Thus the emphasis in practice was to achieve a special state of mind—in other words, to feel and to be different in a significant way. It's worth asking ourselves whether the hope of enlightenment motivates us, even in subtle ways, such as expecting a breakthrough experience to relieve us of our difficulties.

One of the things that many of us *did* learn was that it was certainly possible to have opening or so-called enlightenment experiences, where it was clear that all is one, or that all is love. But it was equally clear that these moments of insight rarely lasted very long, nor did they have a significant residual effect. In other words, the experiences were not permanent, nor did we change very much as a result of having them.

Some people found this very discouraging, and once the magical promise was gone, they left practice altogether. Some of us were fortunate enough to see through the illusion that we brought with us: namely, that if we practiced long and hard enough, we would be permanently free from difficulties. This illusion, which is so typical of our tendency toward black-or-white thinking, has to be seen through before real practice can take hold, since genuine practice is never black or white. The truths in practice are almost always based on paradox, such as the fact that while everything is a mess, all is still well. Practice is also lived in a world of continuums and change, where nothing is permanent—including enlightenment. In fact, rethinking the idea of enlightenment makes much more sense in terms of a continuum—or perhaps we could say "gradual enlightening." This highlights the gradual nature of awakening, rather than reifying it as a permanent state.

What does gradual enlightening actually mean? First, it means becoming increasingly free from the attachment to the prison of our persona, with its deeply ingrained conditioned patterns. This is why practice has to focus, in part, on awareness of our own individual psychology. This means bringing mindfulness to our thoughts in order to see where we're stuck in rigid beliefs about ourselves and about life. For example, everyone has some version of the belief that they're fundamentally not enough in some way. For some, this may take the form of "I'm unworthy." For others the belief may be "I'm flawed." These beliefs are like a lens filter on a camera; they color how we interpret and relate to reality, and consequently dictate how we feel and act. Until we see such beliefs clearly, they will guarantee our unhappiness. Becoming free of such deeply believed thoughts is one of the key steps in the process of gradual enlightening.

Likewise, we need to see through our deeply conditioned emotional reactions, and the behavior patterns that come out of them. Again, this is sometimes viewed as the realm of psychology, but working with our anger and anxiety, or working with our addictions and escapes, is not just a psychological process. It requires meticulous mindfulness and unrelenting honesty with ourselves. And the fruit of this work—as we become increasingly less dominated by our anger, anxiety, and the many related unskillful behavior patterns—is freedom from the burden of our conditioning. This is sometimes called "working with our Me-stuff," and it's certainly part of what it means to become more awake.

Apart from freedom from being caught in our personal psychological conditioning, gradual enlightening has a second key component. This is where we gradually become free from our very limited bubble of perception. Normally we think we see reality, but what we see is our own subjective perceptions, filtered through all of our associations and desires, as well as through language and conditioning. We create this bounded world in order to survive and make sense of things, yet when we live only in our bubble of perception, only in the solid world of fixed boundaries, we are cut off from the totality, the mystery of our being. This is why we cultivate awareness of physical reality—to gradually open into a wider and more spacious awareness. Starting with mindfulness of the breath, and then increasingly opening out of our limited bubble into what is sometimes called "Being Awareness," we can perhaps have occasional tastes of the vastness. As the curtain of separation lifts, we begin to understand that we are more than just our thoughts or just our body. As this understanding gradually develops, we begin to experience, within ourselves, the connectedness that life truly is. The lifetime process of deepening this understanding is an essential aspect of gradual enlightening.

The third aspect of gradual enlightening is the long process of becoming free from living with a closed and disconnected heart. When we begin practice, we are normally so caught up in our separate self—with all of our stories, complaints, entitlements, and desires—that we can rarely get in touch with the love or appreciation that reflect our true nature. This is why we cultivate awareness of the heart, including emphasizing the importance of living from gratitude, loving-kindness, and compassion. The cultivation of these qualities takes time, and it requires that we work with all the internal barriers that get in the way. Yet there is nothing more satisfying in practice than dropping our self-centeredness and learning to live from kindness and an open heart. As much as anything, this awakening of the heart is part of the process of gradual enlightening.

An essential aspect of living more awake is to leave the myths and oversimplifications about enlightenment behind. As Thich Nhat Hanh said, "The real miracle is not to fly or walk on fire. The real miracle is to walk on the Earth, and you could perform that miracle any time." When we understand this, the threefold path of gradual enlightening can begin: first, becoming free of identification with our persona; second, expanding out from our limited bubble of perception; and third, no longer living from a closed and disconnected heart. Understanding this process is part of having a bigger view of what we're doing. Yet the question remains as to why it's so difficult to make a consistent effort to get in touch with a bigger view of practice. The answer, in part, is that sleep and resistance are an integral part of being human—it's our unfortunate mis-wiring. In other words, conditioning cannot be taken lightly. Nor can we ignore that humans will by nature move toward what is comfortable and safe. So it makes sense that we will naturally want to stay in our familiar but very small view of life.

Given this difficulty, what can be done to transform our myopic view to a bigger one? Sometimes, when I walk along the ocean, the Bigger Picture is perfectly apparent. I don't have to think about it, nor is there a need to put it into words. Looking at the ocean and the sky, feeling the magnitude and wonder, there is a clear sense of the connectedness of all and everything. The emotional component can only be described as Love. But it's not personal love—it's the Love that is the nature of our being. Unfortunately, most of the time things are not this clear. This is why we need to find ways to help cultivate the more inclusive view. For some, reading may provide inspiration. This includes books on spiritual practice as well as certain novels that can touch us in unique ways and feed the part of us that aspires to awaken. Regularly going to meditation retreats, where we have the opportunity to go deeper into our practice, also sets up the context for us to occasionally tap into a bigger view.

I've also found that traveling, when done in a particular way, can be very effective in getting us out of our small view of

things. Traveling takes us out of the familiar, and if we can consciously be open to a new environment and circumstances, we
can sometimes break out of our narrow protections and experience life in a bigger context. For example, Elizabeth and I go
overseas once a year for a combination retreat/vacation. We
usually stay away from the tourist attractions and instead spend
our time visiting churches, parks, and on occasion old cemeteries. We go to at least one church each day, just to take in the
wordless reverence of the mystery. Simply sitting in the old ca-
thedrals quietly meditating can be food for our Being. Likewise,
visiting parks is also good "food"—the sanity and simplicity of
being surrounded by natural beauty can generate a deepened
gratitude for life. The gratitude and appreciation for life is deepened even further in some of the old cemeteries. Many of the
gravestones go back hundreds of years, and are visceral reminders that time swiftly passes by. It doesn't feel at all morose, especially since the old cemeteries are often an aesthetic delight—the
stones are all different sizes and shapes, and many are almost falling over. We find it a nice visual reminder that we don't have
endless time.

The point is that to live truly authentically requires opening
out of our small, myopic view of life. Cultivating a Bigger Picture can involve many levels, starting with learning to see every
experience in our life as an opportunity to live more awake.
From there, as we become increasingly free of identification
with our small self, we can begin to expand beyond our limited
bubble of perception into a more openhearted relation to life.
Ultimately, cultivating a bigger view leads to a comprehension
of who we truly are—that the nature of our being is connectedness and love. Living from this understanding is the essence of
living authentically.

17

The Song of Meditation

A famous Zen master sat in meditation every morning listening to two birds jabbering back and forth. As he listened more closely, he would hear the first bird sing, "Tweedley-doo," and the second bird would reply, "Tweedley-dee." A few seconds would pass and they would repeat the same little song, again and again. After a while, as he was sitting more deeply in meditation, he began to hear the first bird sing, "Be here," and the second bird reply, "Just be." Over and over he would hear the Song of Meditation: "Be here. Just be."

This is the essence of sitting meditation, whether it's done sitting cross-legged on a cushion, sitting on a chair, or even lying down. This is the Song of Meditation: "Be here. Just be." The way we learn to sing this song is actually quite simple. We pause. We breathe. We just be. Yet just because this is a simple practice doesn't mean it's easy. In fact, as anyone who has tried meditation has found out, letting ourselves just be is one of the hardest things we will ever do.

The most basic instruction is to sit still and try to be present.

We watch all of the mind's activity as it arises, including the mindless daydreams, the compulsion to plan, the conversations, even the moments of spacing out. We just watch all of it. The idea is to allow whatever arises in awareness to arise unopposed. In fact, if possible, we invite it in—we welcome it. We even welcome our resistance to being present. We let all of it come up and then just watch it.

Often things will come up that we don't like. When this happens, it's particularly helpful to remember that these thoughts and feelings can be our teacher, in that we can learn from them. We don't have to fight them or treat them like an enemy. In other words, we don't try to change our experience or get rid of it—we just try to be aware. Observing ourselves in this way only requires observing, not judging and analyzing, which actually impede the process. When we inevitably begin to judge or analyze, the observing mind takes a step back and just watches those tendencies. This is the mind of curiosity, which can watch our experience unfold without trying to make ourselves or our experience different.

It's interesting to watch what usually happens when we sit down to meditate. The mind will often be busy, jumping from one thing to another. We may react to this busy mind with self-judgment, such as believing that we're not a very good meditator. This is often followed by the thought that we need to do something to fix the situation. This is a very common process; we perceive a problem, the judging mind deems it as bad, and the fixing mind tries to do something about it.

But there's an alternative way to approach our so-called problems. Regardless of what arises during meditation and regardless of how we may be feeling about it, the practice remains the same: we *recognize* what's going on, we *refrain* from getting pulled into it, and then we *return* to being present—letting our experience just be. This requires the basic understanding that our states of mind are not problems to be solved or obstacles to be overcome. Just because something may seem to be wrong, it doesn't mean that it is wrong; it only means that we're adding a judgment to our experience—we're acting out of our expectations of how things *should* be. This inability to let our experience just be causes us endless difficulties.

For example, if we're emotionally upset during a meditation, we will often think that we have to settle down. The truth is, regardless of what we're experiencing, all we need do is be aware of our spinning thoughts and our emotional agitation, do our best to refrain from feeding them, and feel them as the physical experience of the present moment. Again, the basic principle is to simply be aware, and let our experience just be. However, this is not a passive approach; we still need the discipline to stay attentive, and be precise in our observations. This requires an objective curiosity that's willing to look at and be open to whatever arises. It also requires ceasing our resistance to what is, because eventually *everything* will come up, including the things we haven't wanted to see. Yet as we learn to observe our various neuroses and idiosyncrasies without judging them, we begin to view them with benign tolerance. Perhaps we can even laugh at the absurdity of our all-too-human behavior. Learning to be able to laugh at ourselves is one of the many benefits of a meditation practice, and it is also part of the path of living genuinely. We can be serious on the path without being grim.

It's worth repeating that this practice, although in a way very simple, is also very difficult to do. Why? Because the mind is simply not inclined to let things be. It wants to hold on to its opinions and judgments of how things *should* be. The small mind would rather analyze and blame, and there's often a compulsion to find ways to control and fix our experience so that we can feel better. However, as we learn to let our experience just be, it gradually becomes clear that we don't have to feel *any* particular way. This understanding is the essence of inner freedom, and it's an integral part of what it means to live most genuinely.

One problem with just watching our experience and letting it be is that there is sometimes the tendency for sitting practice to become amorphous or spacey. That is why it's so important to stay focused. To help with this, the practice is to rest the mind in the breath and to feel it fully. It is also to rest the mind in the environment—feeling the air, hearing the sounds, sensing the spaciousness of the room. Whenever we drift off into daydreaming or thinking, we use the breath and the environment as anchors to help bring us back to the reality of the present moment. In using these anchors, however, we hold to them lightly, so that we can still let our experience just be. The more we can refrain from trying to control our experiences, the more we can rest our minds in the silence—a silence that is big enough to include the endless mental chatter. It's important to note that we are not *trying* to enter the silence; we enter through the constant soft effort of just being here.

Learning to reside in the stillness, the silence, of *just being* allows us to taste the sweetness of doing nothing. This is not a state of passivity or laziness. The deeper sweetness of doing nothing requires an ability to be at home with ourselves, no longer trying to fill up an inner absence through staying busy or seeking pleasure. Interestingly, "doing nothing" still requires that we make efforts, lots of efforts, and that we make them for a very long time. Nonetheless, in making the soft effort to just be, we are not trying to do or to accomplish anything in particular. In other words, we are giving up our endless effort to control who we are and what we feel. The willingness to just be means exactly that—that we're willing to have things be as they are.

This doesn't mean we can do whatever we want. We still have to refrain from harming ourselves and others. But instead of trying to change what we don't like within ourselves, we're willing instead to observe it, feel it fully, and let it be as it is. For example, when we get angry, we first have to recognize that we're angry. And we certainly have to refrain from expressing it—acting it out—either in actions or in words. This is where a behavioral effort is, in fact, necessary. But once we refrain, the effort is much softer. It's to return to the experience of what anger actually is. This entails observing the thoughts that are trying to grab our attention and physically feeling the energy of anger coursing through the body. We don't have to judge the anger as bad or try to get rid of it. Instead, with the warmth of a gentle curiosity, we observe it as simply deep conditioning playing itself out. And then we let it be.

Because letting ourselves be as we are is not easy, one way of approaching it is to do it piecemeal. For example, to work with our tendency to want to control everything, we can start by learning to let the breath be as it is. Instead of trying to control the breath—to slow it down or make it be smooth or deep—we let the breath breathe itself. Even if it's shallow and erratic, we simply feel what that is.

The following guided meditation is one I've adapted from Stephen Levine. I did this meditation every day for over a year when I was very ill. Sometimes I would ask Elizabeth or one of my daughters to read it to me. Since then I've changed many of the lines to fit with my current practice understanding. The bigger point of this meditation is to actually experience what it is to give up control and just be, and to experience the equanimity of dwelling in the heart of awareness.

Meditation on Letting Be

Adjust your posture so that you are relaxed and alert.

Now bring the attention to the breath.

Not to the thought of the breath but to the actual sensations of breathing.

Feel the body inflate and deflate as you breathe in and out.

Feel the rhythm of the breath. Let yourself breathe naturally without controlling it in any way.

Let the breath be as it is. If it's rapid or erratic, don't try to change it. If it's slow, let it be slow. If it's shallow, let it be shallow.

Let the breath be natural—the breath breathing itself.

All we need to do is to be aware—be aware of the sensations and rhythm of the breathing on its own.

If you notice the mind trying to control the breath in any way, notice that tendency and let the breath be free.

Let the breath be completely as it is.

The breath breathes itself—there's nothing to do.

Just awareness. Spacious as the sky.

Other sensations may arise in awareness. The hands resting in the lap. The tension in the face. The energy flowing through the body. Just notice the sensations and let them be.

No need to label or judge—just experience whatever is there directly.

Sensations of the breath. Sensations of the body. Just moments of experience, appearing and disappearing. Just being.

Notice how thoughts arise. Commenting, judging, thinking—each thought a little bubble, passing through the spaciousness of the mind. Existing for a moment, then dissolving back into the flow.

Thoughts think themselves. There's no need to push them away. Let the thoughts just be.

Let the thought bubbles arise and pass away.

There's nothing to do but be. Softly opening into awareness itself.

Now let awareness expand to include the air around you. The sounds. The light and shadows.

Awareness of breath. Awareness of environment. No need to control.

Letting the breath continue to breathe itself, feel the breath in the center of the chest.

Going deeper into the heart with each in-breath.

There's no one to be. Just breath. Just heart.

An instant of thought. Of judging. Of remembering. Of feeling. Like waves, rising for an instant and dissolving back into the ocean of awareness.

Let each instant unfold as it will.

No resistance anywhere. Resting in the heart, let the breath go right through you.

There's no one special to be—this instant is enough.

Nowhere to go—just now. Just here.

Nothing to do—just be.

Staying with the rhythm and sensations of the breath, residing in the heart of awareness, let life be as it is.

Learning to let life just be is one of the most important efforts we have to make in practice. But it's a soft effort—the kind of effort that's described in the Song of Meditation: "Be here. Just be." Here we learn to dwell in the heart of awareness, giving up the requirement that we feel a particular way. Learning to let life be as it is and to be at home in our own skins is one of the most satisfying benefits of living authentically.

18

The Most Important Thing

When Elizabeth and I were in Rome, we came across an old church called Santa Maria della Concezione dei Cappuccini, beneath which lies what's known as the Capuchin Crypt. When the monks arrived there in 1631, they brought three hundred cartloads of the bones of deceased monks and proceeded to arrange the bones in decorative motifs throughout the several underground chapels. It's quite a sight, but the thing that struck me the most was a phrase on the wall above some of the bones: "What you are now we used to be; what we are now you will be." It was a particularly effective wake-up to what's most important.

I imagine Alfred Nobel had a similar wake-up when he opened the newspaper to find his own obituary in it. It may have been doubly shocking because the obituary stated, "Alfred Nobel, the inventor of dynamite, died this week." It was actually his brother who had died, but what was most upsetting to Alfred was the realization that he would be remembered for inventing dynamite. The shock of this realization motivated him to reflect on what he considered to be most important. As a result of his reflections he sponsored what came to be known as the Nobel Peace Prize. Sobered by reading his premature obituary, he thenceforth put his time, money, and energy into supporting what he valued most—people who were learning to live from the awaked heart, as evidenced by their pursuit of world peace.

When I reflect on what I consider to be the most important thing, the answer I keep returning to is learning to live from the gratitude and kindness of the awakened heart. Unfortunately this is not so easy to do; often, to awaken the heart, we first have to experience adversity. We may have to lose things we cherish, where we feel our secure future dissolving right in front of us. There's a famous story about the wife of a wealthy man whose sorrow was so great when her only child died that she came close to losing her mind. Someone told her to talk to the Buddha. The Buddha told her that he could help her, but first she had to bring him some white mustard seeds from a family where no one had died. She desperately went from house to house, but everywhere she went someone had died. At first she was disappointed, but then it struck her that no one was spared the loss of someone they loved. When she returned to the Buddha, she was able to relate to her sorrow with compassion for others as well as for herself. It was the beginning of moving from self-centeredness to the awakening of the heart.

When we experience great difficulty, either on a societal or on a personal level, it often helps break down our self-protectiveness and sense of separation. There are many historical examples on a societal level—from World War II, 9/11, and others—where people come together in shared purpose and shared heart when faced with overwhelming adversity. This is certainly true on the individual level as well. When we consciously face our deepest tragedies or suffering, we often feel a sense of connectedness with others who are in pain. Like the woman who went to see the Buddha, we can begin to appreciate our common humanity. The experience of "my pain" is transformed into "the pain"—the pain all human beings share. This is the essence and definition of compassion.

One particular difficulty, which is one of the most effective catalysts to awakening the heart, is experiencing the pain of remorse. Sometimes we get a glimpse of the fact that we're living from vanity or unkindness or pettiness, and we feel a cringe of conscience. This is the experience of remorse, which arises when we become acutely aware that we are going against our true nature—against the heart that seeks to awaken. We can feel the pain we cause others, as well as ourselves; and this experience is almost always sobering. In fact, perhaps as much as anything, the pain of remorse can motivate a profound desire within us to live more awake and more genuinely. From the pain of deep humiliation—from seeing how we go against our true nature—real humility can awaken. Several years ago I had an experience of remorse that had a profound impact on my practice. While I was sitting on a bench overlooking the ocean doing a loving-kindness meditation, a woman who appeared to be homeless came over to talk to me. But after a minute or so I told her I was busy meditating. Do you get it? I was too busy doing a meditation on kindness to extend actual kindness to a person who may have been in need.

As soon as she went away, I felt the shock of remorse. This was not guilt, which is usually based in anger against oneself, but rather the awareness that I'd disconnected from the heart. By allowing myself to truly feel this, to let it etch its way into my awareness without indulging in self-blame, I saw the gap between my ideals about living from kindness, and having kindness be a lived reality. Because the experience of remorse was so intense, it had a residual impact that has stayed with me. Now when I find myself at that choice point between extending myself with kindness, or holding back from laziness or self-protection, I am more likely to live from the natural generosity of the heart.

An interesting and sometimes very fruitful exercise in consciously experiencing remorse is to image what might be written on your tombstone. Just like the wake-up that Alfred Nobel experienced when he realized he might be remembered as the inventor of dynamite, we can be equally sobered when we see what we might be remembered for. Would we want our tombstone to say, "He was angry and he died." Or, "She held on to her resentments until her dying day." Or, "He died never having given back." These may be exaggerations, but we all have big lapses in which we forget what is most important. The point is that we don't have to wait until our death to remember. We can use our "little deaths"—those moments when we see that we're being petty, unkind, or unforgiving—to remind us that the most important thing is to live from the gratitude and kindness of the awakening heart. For example, if we're caught in holding on to resentment, we can bring to mind Black Elk's words: "It is in the darkness in our own eyes that men lose their way." With the pain of remorse, this realization can help us to move out of our self-centeredness and into a more open and genuine way of living.

Remorse is one path to awakening to what is most important. Another is through the intentional cultivation of gratitude. Our culture, which is based in self-centeredness, does not actually foster the natural cultivation of this feeling. Gratitude may be given lip service, such as the moral dictate that we *should* be thankful, but in reality, we're taught to protect "Me and Mine." This is not true in every culture. There's an African tribe where an anthropologist proposed a game to the children. He put a basket full of fruit near a tree and told the children that whoever got there first won the sweet fruits. When he told them to run, they all took each other's hands and ran together, then sat together enjoying their treats. When he asked them why they had run like that when one of them could have had all the fruits for himself, they said, "*Ubuntu*, how can one of us be happy if all the other ones are sad?" "Ubuntu" in their culture means, "I am because we are."

Even though gratitude is an intrinsic aspect of the awakened heart, we often have to work with the barriers that prevent us from connecting with it—barriers such as selfishness, fear, and self-protectiveness. One way to work with these barriers, and to cultivate our natural gratitude, is to do a daily gratitude practice called Nightly Reflection. Many have found this practice helpful, not only in cultivating gratitude but also in opening to the experience of remorse. In a way, these two go together: the more we experience remorse for living from a closed heart, the more we aspire to live from gratitude.

The Practice of Nightly Reflection

Nightly Reflection is a relaxed meditation that is done right before going to sleep. I do it lying on my back in bed with my hands folded on my stomach. The eyes can be open or closed. It's best to do this at approximately the same time each night, and it's especially important to do before getting too tired.

The intention of Nightly Reflection is to review the events of the day, starting from your first memory of the morning to the moment you began your evening's practice. Focus on the main events—the thoughts and feelings you experienced throughout the day—as if you were watching a movie. During

Nightly Reflection, it's important not to get pulled into thinking, analyzing, or judging, but instead to review what actually transpired as objectively as possible. The instruction is to try to stay physically grounded by maintaining awareness of the breath in the area of the center of the chest. Without this grounding, the exercise can easily become too mental.

Once the review is finished, ask yourself two questions: "What am I most thankful for?" and "What do I feel the most remorse for?" Note that breathing into the center of the chest is particularly important when we are raising these two questions, since it helps avoid the mental detours of thinking and judging.

In doing the Nightly Reflection regularly, we become not only more appreciative during the meditation, we also become more aware and receptive during the day. For example, we begin to notice that we are often not very appreciative as we go through our daily routine. Little positive moments are often not even acknowledged or, if so, are quickly forgotten. But as we become more attuned to what is actually happening during the day, these moments begin to stand out, and we experience genuine appreciation during the present-moment experience.

Similarly, in asking what we are most remorseful about each evening, our sensitivity to this also becomes much more finely tuned during the day. Interestingly, when we can simply notice, without judging ourselves, where we feel remorse, it is not at all discouraging. In fact, feeling this awakening of conscience is very positive and helps activate the aspiration to live from the awakened heart. In effect, by reviewing our day through a focused Nightly Reflection practice, we're remembering what is most important. Watching the movie clip of the long body of our day allows us to see what we do more objectively, while at the same time being much less identified with it. This, in turn, allows us to open to a bigger sense of things.

KINDNESS

Along with gratitude, one other essential aspect of living from the awakened heart is kindness. In fact, when asked what he considered to be the most important thing, the Dalai Lama answered, "Kindness." Kindness, like gratitude, needs to be cultivated. But to have the discipline to cultivate kindness, we may first need to realize how often we are incapable of extending it. A Hospice patient once said to me, "Knowing I have cancer and probably only a short time to live gives me a certain freedom to say things I wouldn't have said before." She said it not as a justification to vent her anger and tell people off, but to describe her growing courage to be honest and genuine. She realized how she often held back her heart, either from laziness or fear or self-doubt. It took the awareness of the fact that her time was limited for her to be able to live more authentically.

When we find ourselves in situations where we see the choice point between self-centeredness and extending kindness, we can remember the question of the eternal recurrence: "If I were to live my life in the exact same way, again and again and again, throughout eternity, what would I do in this situation?" This question is a direct call to awakening the heart, and the answer will turn us away from self-centeredness and toward kindness. It will remind us of what is truly the most important thing.

Once we're aware of how crucial it is to aspire to live from kindness, we're ready to begin the actual work of cultivating it. One way to cultivate it on a daily basis is through the Loving-kindness Meditation. There are many different versions of this meditation, but the essence is to extend unconditional friendliness, both to ourselves and to others. It's about living from the awakened heart, where we naturally desire the welfare of everyone. The one thing that most prevents our natural loving-kindness from coming forth is the solidity of the judgmental mind—finding fault with both ourselves and others. And the one most effective way to undercut this tendency to judge is through staying grounded in the breath in and out of the heart, while at the same time saying words to direct our attention toward awakening our natural wish for the well-being of everyone. Here are the instructions:

Loving-kindness Meditation

Either sitting in meditation posture or lying down in a comfortable position, begin by taking a couple of deep breaths. Become aware of the breath and begin to follow it into the center of the chest, relaxing into the body. Experience the area around the heart. Whatever you feel, just be aware of that. With each in-breath let awareness go a little deeper.

To activate the quality of loving-kindness, first think of someone for whom you have very positive feelings. Picture them. Breathe them in on the heart-breath. Let your innate loving-kindness be activated.

TOWARD ONESELF

Now shift the focus to yourself, and stay with each of the following lines for a few breaths:

Breathing in, dwelling in the heart.
Breathing out, extending loving-kindness to myself, exactly as I am right now.

Relate with a benign friendliness to wherever you may be caught in your conditioning, including the self-judgments of being flawed or lacking. If there is no warmth, no loving-kindness to extend, simply notice this and continue.

Breathing in, dwelling in the heart.
Breathing out, no one special to be.

Feel the momentary freedom of no longer living from pretense or images of how you should be or feel, including the need to feel special or loving.

Breathing in, dwelling in the heart.
Breathing out, just being.

Drop the need to struggle, to get somewhere, to prove yourself; feel the spaciousness and lightness of heart of living from your natural Being.

Repeat the above lines two more times.

TOWARD OTHERS

Now think of someone close to you, for whom you wish to extend loving-kindness. Breathe the person's image into the center of your chest on the in-breath. On the out-breath extend loving-kindness to this person while repeating the following three lines. If you feel resistance, just acknowledge it and experience whatever is in the way.

Breathing [name] in,
May you dwell in the heart.

Breathing [name] in,
May you be healed in your difficulties.

Breathing [name] in,
May your heart be open to others.

Repeat these lines, inserting the names of any other people you'd like to include in this meditation.

TOWARD EVERYONE

Finally, expand your awareness to include everyone. Bring this awareness into the center of your chest with the in-breath, and with the out-breath repeat the following three lines, allowing loving-kindness to be extended to everyone:

Breathing everyone in,
May you dwell in the heart.

Breathing everyone in,
May you be healed in your difficulties.

Breathing everyone in,
May your hearts be open to others.

TO END THE MEDITATION

Repeat the first line of this practice, "*Breathing in, dwelling in the heart,*" relaxing into the heartfelt sense of just being.

The Loving-kindness Meditation is perhaps the single most transformative meditation practice I have ever encountered. However, for it to take root in our lives, it needs to be done on a daily basis. The good news is that when we do it regularly, it gradually becomes not just an exercise but our natural response to life. It allows us to *live* from what is most important. We may first have to experience adversity and loss, as well as remorse. We may also need to persevere for a long time in our efforts to cultivate gratitude and kindness, but living from the awakened heart is the essence of living authentically. And it's the fruition of discovering who we most truly are.

19

Enjoy the Ride

For an eleven-year period, ending when I was in my forties, I lived on a rural property with my wife and two young daughters. We had a half-acre organic garden and tried to grow most of our own food, including raising chickens, sheep, and goats. What we didn't know was that the prior owners had buried DDT and other toxic farm chemicals right where we had our garden and pasture; so for eleven years we were filling our bodies with poison. We didn't discover this until my wife and I both got very sick with an immune system disease, and although we moved, there was no cure for the disease, only symptomatic relief with the aid of powerful steroids.

Before I got sick, although I had a fairly stable meditation practice, it had been clear to me for a while that I was somewhat stuck in the complacency of the familiar, with nothing pushing me to go deeper. This changed radically with the onset of the severe symptoms of weakness, pain, and an unrelenting feeling of nausea. At first I could no longer sit in meditation, since I lacked both physical energy and mental clarity, and for a period of a few months I felt lost and groundless. Yet as often happens when we are faced with intense difficulty and uncertainty, this illness was a pivotal turning point in my practice and in my life. At first haltingly, and later with a genuine willingness, I learned to relate to my physical condition in a new way; and in the process I also learned how to truly enjoy the ride.

Many people talk about viewing their illnesses as a gift. However, when I first got sick, I saw it as just the opposite—as an unwanted obstacle that I wanted to get rid of as soon as possible. The result of resisting my life was anger, anxiety, confusion, depression, and isolation. My attachments to comfort and control, both of which ran very deep, were severely challenged. Yet for whatever reasons, instead of giving up and wallowing in despair, this most difficult circumstance became the most fruitful learning experience I had ever had up until then. The learning began when I was able to reframe my resistance to the illness so that I could see it as my path—particularly my path to freedom from attachment. This reframing did not come quickly or easily, but at one point the depth of my misunderstanding became very clear: I may not like my experience and I can try to push it away, but the fact remains that whatever is happening right now, regardless of how unpleasant it is, is my genuine life. Whether or not the small mind wants it is not the point; to live most authentically requires that we honestly embrace our life, exactly as it is.

Being able to see our most difficult experiences as our path means that we understand, very specifically, how our difficulty pushes us to work with the exact places where we are most caught in our attachments. For example, one of the places I was particularly caught was in my emotion-based thoughts— thoughts such as "Poor me," "This isn't how it was supposed to be," "What's going to happen to me?" "I can't take this." These layers and layers of believed thoughts were at first very intractable, but in repeatedly observing the mind and labeling the thoughts each time they arose, it made it possible to be able to observe the thoughts without getting caught in them, and it began to feel as if age-old excess baggage was dropping away.

Another deeply believed thought had been that I was in control. Before I got sick, I led a very active and physical life. After I got sick, I had no control, no choice but to slow down and be largely inactive. At first it seemed depressing—sometimes it felt like my life was over. I had been caught in the illusion of being in control and also that I had endless time. As these illusions began to be dispelled, I couldn't imagine what was going to happen. Yet the more I could see the illness as my path, the more I could appreciate the depths of awareness that are possible when we slow down enough to let life in. I could actually feel the texture of my life, and I began to see how staying busy and believing I was in control were in many ways props. Giving up the illusion of control, at least to some extent, allowed me to feel grateful for the equanimity of doing simple mundane activities, including sitting around, not doing anything in particular.

We all have many attachments, and one of the strongest is no doubt to our body, especially to our feeling of comfort. This was one of my biggest challenges—wanting to feel a particular way, and also *not* wanting to feel a particular way, namely nauseous and in pain. Because the nausea was somewhat unrelenting and because I didn't want to take the toxic drugs that could mask it, I learned how to stay present with it without adding the story of "This is awful." Sometimes the only thing I could do was lie in the fetal position, and as often as I was able, I would breathe into the area of the heart on the in-breath and then extend loving-kindness to my body, to my immune system, via the out-breath.

Dwelling deeply in the heart, I found I could enter directly into the experience of the nausea, not as "pain" but as intense physical energy. No longer needing to feel a particular way, I was sometimes struck by a sense of the quiet joy of just being. In giving up my attachment to comfort I would sometimes feel a depth of appreciation that, by any ordinary standards, simply did not compute.

My other strongest attachments were to my identities—husband, father, breadwinner, meditator, athlete, and so forth—and it was very disconcerting watching my life as I had known it begin to fall apart. But again, in seeing this new situation as my path to becoming free, my whole world turned right side up. As I would experience the groundlessness of having lost my identities, I would breathe the arising fear right into the center of the chest on the in-breath and simply feel it. The more I could stay present with the uncertainty, the more the illusory self-images would be stripped away. There were moments when I experienced the freedom of not *needing* to be anyone at all. By letting everything I was clinging to just fall apart, without much choice in the matter, I found that what remained was more than enough.

I mentioned earlier that one of the things I experienced with the onset of my illness was the feeling of isolation. Even though there were people who cared for me, I nonetheless felt very alone. The world of intense physical discomfort, along with the fear of the loss of my life as I had known it, combined to create a subjective reality that seemed grim and disconnected. But interestingly, the more I was able to truly open to and feel the discomfort and loss—minus the melodrama—the more I began to tap into a sense of compassion for others in pain. I wasn't actually trying to do this; yet as the illness pushed me to explore the roots of my own fears, it became clear to me how many others were suffering with even worse conditions, and compassion for those in pain came forth naturally. This wasn't an intellectual understanding; it was an experiential process born out of the inner realization of the pain that all human beings share. With this realization and sense of connection with others the feelings of isolation completely disappeared.

As soon as I had a period of improved health, I became a Hospice volunteer, not out of an idealized vision that I could help others who were dying but to help me stay in touch with this newly discovered sense of connection and compassion—and also as a reminder that our time is limited. Despite my numerous breakthroughs in working with my attachments, I knew how quickly my old patterns would try to reestablish themselves when my symptoms would go into remission. In fact, over the years it has been a constant struggle to remind myself not to fall back into complacency. Although I never felt in imminent danger of dying, I realized that it's still a kind of death when we live out of complacency and fear—not wanting to let go of the comfort of the familiar. But fortunately, even when I experience fairly long periods of remission from my symptoms, there are still days when my body is in such discomfort that all I can do is lie down for hours on end. This is fortunate, because it forces me once again to stay truly present with the physical experience. Interestingly, sometimes it almost feels as if I'm floating in awareness itself; the nausea and discomfort remain, but it almost isn't me. In these moments there's a clear awareness that who we are is more than just this body. This is just one example of what I have had to learn over and over again—that to live truly authentically means being willing to welcome the unwanted and to embrace uncertainty. We can come to understand that pain and loss, when consciously welcomed, can greatly accelerate our ability to be free from our attachments.

Perhaps more than anything, my adventure with illness has shown me how freedom from our deeply held attachments—to comfort, control, our identities, to a predictable future—can lead to a life of genuine appreciation. Nowhere is this more true than in our attachment to those we love. Part of appreciating those we are closest to has to include the awareness that our time together is limited. We have no idea what will happen, or when, which is again the theme of skating on thin ice. But this fact doesn't have to make us morose. In fact, knowing that our time is limited allows us to appreciate one another all the more. I remember a few years ago when Elizabeth and I were on a wonderful retreat-vacation in the beautiful area of Lake Como, in northern Italy. We spent hours walking through idyllic little towns, eating pasta at almost every meal, meditating in a different church each day, and appreciating how lucky we were to have the health and resources to share our life together. Then, shortly after our return to San Diego, Elizabeth was diagnosed with breast cancer.

Even though Elizabeth responded to this with very little melodrama, I nonetheless remember feeling as if the ground had been pulled out from under me. And in spite of my many years of practicing with my own illness, I couldn't deny that I was still somewhat caught up in the illusion that we had endless time. This illusion, which we all have to some degree, leaves us convinced that our life will continue indefinitely into the vague future. We are rarely aware of the extent to which this belief keeps us skating on thin ice, oblivious of the very real fact that our lives can end or be drastically altered at any time, without any warning.

Yet the fact that we are inexorably getting older makes it increasingly difficult to maintain our illusion of endless time. We hear about more and more people we know being diagnosed with cancer or some other serious condition, and it is no longer unusual for someone close to us to die. We can continue to try to ignore the evidence, but nonetheless the cracks in the thin ice seem to get bigger with each loss. We may think it's not fair, but that's just the point of view of the small mind of ego—the sense of entitlement that life should go the way we want it to go. Interestingly, in historical perspective, our times are actually relatively safe and comfortable, and perhaps that fortifies the illusion of control. Yet it can seem daunting when this illusion is shattered, as it was for me with Elizabeth's diagnosis.

As we become increasingly aware that we and our loved ones have limited time, we are bound to have times of feeling groundless and disconnected. I certainly felt the fear of disconnection and loss when I was told Elizabeth had cancer. But we can't forget that true connection comes when we're willing to acknowledge these uncomfortable feelings that are part of our human condition. True connection comes when we breathe the aching fear of loss into the center of our chests and simply let it be there, no matter how uncomfortable we might feel. Once we truly learn to reside in our fear of aloneness, we will no longer expect those close to us to take away our fears. Instead we will know real intimacy, which can never be based on neediness or the fear of being alone. When we relate to people from the small mind of neediness, we can't truly love them or appreciate them.

The fact is, facing our fears exposes our deepest attachments and leaves us without the false props of our illusions. Although this can be painful at times, the good news is that the melodrama doesn't have to take over, and instead we can begin to see through what we are most attached to. If you ask me if I was attached to Elizabeth, the answer was—and is—absolutely! In fact, one of the things that became clear to me was how much I was caught in the belief that I couldn't be happy without her. But dealing with her cancer, and then other subsequent cracks in the thin ice, has helped me to realize the degree of self-centered neediness in my attachment—to her, to her good health, to our life together. Aren't our difficulties always our best teacher, taking us to the places we rarely willingly go on our own? Over the last few years, as I've watched my mind have such thoughts as "I need Elizabeth in order to be happy," it's become clear that these thoughts are based in personal self-interest and fear. And it's also become clear that every one of these thoughts prevents me from really being with Elizabeth, because they're not about her but about me.

Practice helps us open to our feelings of groundlessness and leads us to become more willing to surrender to our fears—such as our fear of the loss of control, the loss of the familiar, even the fear of the loss of a loved one. Residing in our fears without trying to get rid of them or to outrun them is what erodes our attachments and helps us see through our illusions—the illusion that we have endless time, or that we can make life go the way we want, or that we need another person in order to be happy.

How can we face these fears directly? First we must be willing to drop the story line—the thoughts that the spinning mind keeps churning out. Once we refrain from indulging in thoughts such as "This is awful," "I can't handle this," or "Poor me," the melodrama loses its steam, and we're left with something that is much more workable—the actual energy of fear and loss. Then we can say yes to them, which means we are willing to feel them rather than run away from them. It may seem counterintuitive, yet when fear of loss arises, if we breathe the sensations of anxiety right into the center of our chests, we may find that our usual dread is replaced with a genuine curiosity. As the familiar thoughts that normally fuel our fear begin to fall away, we can experience the healing power of the heart. This is a nonconceptual experience—it does not come from words or explanations, but rather from the spaciousness of a wider container of awareness. The fear of living as a separate being dissolves, and we can naturally tap into the connectedness and love that are always available to us. These are the real fruit of the practice life.

The result of all this for me is that I'm now even more appreciative of Elizabeth and more able to be with her fully. It's not that I wasn't appreciative of her before, but being caught in my attachments prevented me from being truly present with her. And perhaps even more so, I'm grateful every day for being able to simply share a life together—not just our practice together but all of the mundane moments as well. This is not to say that I'm now totally free of attachment to her, but my attachment is much more lightly held. Practice can transform our perceived need for a particular person into a less emotion-based preference. Having preferences isn't a problem, nor is enjoying them. The problem is when we're so enslaved by our attachments that they run our lives. But as the demand loses its hold, we can simply enjoy it as a preference.

Of course, no one wants to reside in the sinking groundlessness that is triggered when we fall through one of the cracks in the thin ice. Nonetheless, it's only when we're able to reside in the physical experience of no ground—where we're no longer clinging to our fantasies of how life is supposed to be—that the power of our attachments begins to diminish. Before we can truly live from appreciation, we first have to consciously know loss. This is the path of practice. When we see through our attachments by fully experiencing them, the result is freedom. When we can see and experience life without the filters of our judgments and demands, the result is appreciation and the quiet joy of being. When we see through our fears, the result is love.

Much of this book has been about facing our difficult experiences, looking honestly at our beliefs and strategies, and working with our fears. Are these things difficult? Yes, they're difficult, but more importantly, they're also the path to being able to increasingly enjoy our life. As it says in an old Hungarian proverb: "Life is like licking honey—licking honey off a thorn." We learn to enjoy the honey, in part, *because* of the thorns. Acknowledging the unpleasant, seeing through our delusions, facing our fears, always takes courage—the courage of taking a step even while fear is present. But courage is what ultimately allows us to live most authentically. It allows us to choose freedom, rather than staying caught in complacency and fear.

Over the course of a practice life we may forget this many times and find ourselves going off course. But we can't judge ourselves for each wayward detour. Each detour, each backslide, is actually part of the path of learning and growth. If we are to affirm our life, to say yes to it, we must say yes to *all* of it. Each detour and backslide is an integral part of the whole; would we be who we are today if we hadn't learned from our so-called mistakes and flaws? Living authentically means we're acknowledging the whole of what our life is, and being willing to truly live it, just as it is. The key, of course, is to cease resistance to what is. When I finally understood this in relation to my illness and to Elizabeth's cancer, I became willing to affirm that I was on board for the trip. Whether I liked the trip or not, I could still enjoy the ride—to see what it was like and where it was going, without the extra baggage of self-pity and fear. Self-pity, the complaints and judgments, and especially all of the fears, are the real obstacles to surrendering to what is. They are also what prevent genuine appreciation for our life. This is the kind of appreciation that artist Paul Klee described when he said, "Imagine you are dead. After many years of exile you are permitted to cast a single glance earthward. You see a lamppost and an old dog lifting his leg against it. You are so moved that you cannot stop sobbing."

There is a message that all of us need to hear over and over again: "Time is fleeting. Don't hold back. Appreciate this precious life." The wish of every teacher is for all of us to be able to take these words to heart.

Also by Ezra Bayda

Published by Shambhala Publications

At Home in the Muddy Water: A Guide to Finding Peace within Everyday Chaos (2004)

In this book, Bayda applies the simple Zen teaching of being "at home in the muddy water" to a range of everyday concerns—including relationships, trust, sexuality, and money—showing that everything we need to practice is right here before us, and that peace and fulfillment is available to everyone, right here, right now, no matter what their circumstances.

Being Zen: Bringing Meditation to Life (2002)

We can use whatever life presents, Ezra Bayda teaches, to strengthen our spiritual practice—including the turmoil of daily life. What we need is the willingness to just be with our experiences—whether they are painful or pleasing—opening ourselves to the reality of our lives without trying to fix or change anything. But doing this requires that we confront our most deeply rooted fears and assumptions in order to gradually become free of the constrictions and suffering they create. Then we can awaken to the loving-kindness that is at the heart of our being.

Beyond Happiness: The Zen Way to True Contentment (2010)

Happiness is available to all of us—right here, right now. All that's required is that we learn to let go of our expectation that life should go according the agenda we have in mind. Zen teacher Ezra Bayda provides the teachings and practices we need to learn to let go into true happiness—the kind that goes far deeper than the kind that's about getting what we think we want.

Zen Heart: Simple Advice for Living with Mindfulness and Compassion (2008)

Ezra Bayda's gift for taking Zen teaching and relating it to every aspect of life has made his books popular even with people who aren't Buddhists. In *Zen Heart*, Ezra continues in the mode of his books like *Being Zen* to show how spiritual practice works in everyday life. He breaks spiritual practice down into three basic stages. The phases enrich each other to create a practice that works no matter what the complexities of your circumstances.